Domestic Economic Abuse

Supriya Singh tells the stories of 12 Anglo-Celtic and Indian women in Australia who survived economic abuse. She describes the lived experience of coercive control underlying economic abuse across cultures.

Each story shows how the woman was trapped and lost her freedom because her husband denied her money, appropriated her assets, and sabotaged her ability to be in paid work. These stories are about silence, shame, and embarrassment that this could happen despite professional and graduate education. Some of the women were the main earners in their household. Women spoke of being afraid, of trying to leave, of losing their sense of self. Many suffered physical and mental ill-health, not knowing what would trigger the violence. Some attempted suicide. None of the women fully realised they were suffering family violence through economic abuse, whilst it was happening to them.

The stories of Anglo-Celtic and Indian women show economic abuse is not associated with a specific system of money management and control. It is when the morality of money is betrayed that control becomes coercive. Money as a medium of care then becomes a medium of abuse.

The women's stories demonstrate the importance of talking about money and relationships with future partners, across life stages and with their sons and daughters. The women saw this as an essential step for preventing and lessening economic abuse.

A vital read for scholars of domestic abuse and family violence that will also be valuable for sociologists of money.

Supriya Singh is a sociologist of money, migration and family. She is Honorary Professor at the Graduate School of Business and Law, Royal Melbourne Institute of Technology (RMIT) University.

Routledge Advances in Sociology

316 Anxiety in Middle-Class America
Sociology of Emotional Insecurity in Late Modernity
Valérie de Courville Nicol

317 Boredom and Academic Work
Mariusz Finkielsztein

318 The Emotions in the Classics of Sociology
A Study in Social Theory
Edited by Massimo Cerulo and Adrian Scribano

319 Emotions and Belonging in Forced Migration
Syrian Refugees and Asylum Seekers
Basem Mahmud

320 Languages and Social Cohesion
A Transdisciplinary Literature Review
Gabriela Meier and Simone Smala

321 The Social Construction of the US Academic Elite
A Mixed Methods Study of Two Disciplines
Stephanie Buyer

322 Domestic Economic Abuse
The Violence of Money
Supriya Singh

For more information about this series, please visit: https://www.routledge.com/Routledge-Advances-in-Sociology/book-series/SE0511

Domestic Economic Abuse
The Violence of Money

Supriya Singh

LONDON AND NEW YORK

First published 2022
by Routledge
2 Park Square, Milton Park, Abingdon, Oxon OX14 4RN

and by Routledge
605 Third Avenue, New York, NY 10158

*Routledge is an imprint of the Taylor & Francis Group,
an informa business*

© 2022 Supriya Singh

The right of Supriya Singh to be identified as author of this work has been asserted by her in accordance with sections 77 and 78 of the Copyright, Designs and Patents Act 1988.

All rights reserved. No part of this book may be reprinted or reproduced or utilised in any form or by any electronic, mechanical, or other means, now known or hereafter invented, including photocopying and recording, or in any information storage or retrieval system, without permission in writing from the publishers.

Trademark notice: Product or corporate names may be trademarks or registered trademarks, and are used only for identification and explanation without intent to infringe.

British Library Cataloguing in Publication Data
A catalogue record for this book is available from the British Library

Library of Congress Cataloging in Publication Data
A catalog record for this book has been requested

ISBN: 978-1-032-01430-2 (hbk)
ISBN: 978-1-032-01431-9 (pbk)
ISBN: 978-1-003-17860-6 (ebk)

DOI: 10.4324/9781003178606

Typeset in Times New Roman
by KnowledgeWorks Global Ltd.

This book is dedicated to the women who shared their stories.

Contents

Acknowledgements ix
Preface xi

1 Introduction: Economic abuse is the untold story of family violence 1

2 Carol: The joint account becomes a medium of abuse 24

3 Ekta: The 'good son' sends her money to his parents 31

4 Rina: Dowry is economic, emotional and physical abuse 35

5 Geeta: He gave me coins, not notes 41

6 Karen: 'I've been a single mother for most of my married life' 46

7 Asha: 'You now belong to my family and your money is mine' 53

8 Chitra: He and his family abused her because she did not behave 'like a good wife' 58

9 Prema: He married her to get permanent residence 63

10 Betty: After he died she recognised it as economic abuse 70

11	Heer: She knew she should leave but was in a silent 'cultural bind'	77
12	Bala: A story of torture, survival and empowerment	84
13	Enid: Talking of money	90
14	Conclusion	98
	Index	111

Acknowledgements

My first and most important debt is to the women who agreed to tell and review their stories. The women relived their trauma, even when these stories were 20 years old. It was an act of courage. They trusted me with their experiences hoping some good may come of this telling.

I would like to acknowledge my research partners Associate Professor Marg Liddell of RMIT University and Dr Jasvinder Sidhu of Federation University Australia. We researched 'Money, Gender and Family Violence across Cultures' 2016–2017, from which this narrative is drawn. I would also like to thank Marg for reading and commenting on the final draft.

I also worked closely with Dr Rhonda Cumberland and Rachna Bowman of South East Community Links (SECL) that provides settlement support services for new migrant and refugee communities.

I am indebted to Lyn Richards who has mentored me and read several drafts of this book and others since she supervised my Ph.D. some 30 years ago. For the last four years she has also heard me talk again and again of economic abuse. I thank her for our intellectual intimacy around the study of money and qualitative research.

Margaret Jackson also heard me tell these stories without stop over our fortnightly coffee sessions. John Burke was the first reader of the initial draft and got me writing again when it had spluttered. I am also indebted to Marilyn McMahon and Paul McGorrery for our discussions on criminalising coercive control in Australia. I connected again with Carolyn Bond and Bernadette Pascoe from my early world in consumer finance in Australia. I also reached out to Jan Pahl about studying money and power and to Viviana Zelizer when writing of the morality and relational literacy of money.

I shared some of the early drafts with Anita Anand, Mariel Beros, Glenis Henderson, Toni Magor, Pam Robinson, Dorothy Frei, Manjit Kaur and Shalu Nigam.

Acknowledgements

I would also like to thank Simon Bates of Taylor & Francis for his enthusiasm and belief that writing of economic abuse could make a difference.

In the end, the book was a solitary endeavour. I lived with the stories of the women who had survived economic abuse. They trusted me to tell their stories so that we could address and prevent economic abuse.

Preface

This book aims to raise social awareness about economic abuse, the hidden aspect of family violence. It is also a call for sociologists of money and those studying family violence to work together to better understand money, gender, and coercive control. Policy makers and practitioners can then better understand how economic abuse is shaped by the gender and morality of money across time and cultures.

This book tells the lived experience of 12 Anglo-Celtic and Indian women in Australia who survived economic abuse. The women who told their stories hoped their stories would help other women see and name economic abuse. They had learnt it is important to talk about money and relationships to lessen or avoid the pain and desolation of economic abuse.

I hope this book will lead to major social change through a greater emphasis on the 'relational literacy of money'. This will help us learn how to speak of money with our children and partners across life stages. Talking of money in intimate relationships is difficult for it can unravel issues of power, dependency, and opposing moralities. But talking of money with unconditional mutual regard can also increase intimacy. It can reveal how a person grew up, the kind of intimate relationships he or she wants, and the kind of future they see for themselves.

Each woman's story is different for it is set in her individual biography and changing cultural practices around money in intimate relationships. But each woman's story is also the same, as it is about coercive control that works through isolation, entrapment, and the loss of freedom and human rights.

Economic abuse involves denying women money, sabotaging work, and appropriating assets. The gender of money and morality shapes the experience of economic abuse. The impact is equally devastating across cultures and socio-economic groups, leading to mental and physical ill health, a loss of sense of self and freedom.

I have written the stories of women, for it is women who predominantly suffer economic abuse. Gender inequality and a male sense of entitlement means men are most often the perpetrators.

These stories are particularly important as we live through COVID-19. Increased isolation and the greater economic fragility of women incubate family violence. The pandemic has trapped people together within the house, decreasing opportunities to leave, be supported and survive.

The stories are of Anglo-Celtic and Indian women in Australia because I know these communities best through my research on money in marriage, migration and the family. Placing these stories side by side shows that family violence is not something that happens only in 'other' communities. It happens to one in four women in Australia and one in three globally.

Economic abuse does not only happen to marginalised women. The women in these stories have professional or graduate education. Nearly all were in paid work or had been employed as professionals before marriage. Six of the 12 were the main earners in the household.

I came to know of most of the women through personal and professional networks. Two of the 12 women were introduced by participants. Only two had sought help from a family violence service provider.

One story comes from my 2006–2014 study on 'Money, Migration and Family.'[1] It is this woman's story that led me to ask: How does money as a medium of care become a medium of abuse?

I interviewed 11 of the 12 women as part of a study on 'Money, Gender and Family Violence across Cultures' between 2016 and 2017.[2] The aim of the research was to understand the role of money and gender in family violence across cultures.

The interviews were open-ended and held at a place the woman chose. I conducted the interviews in English, Hindi, and Punjabi. Most

---

1 I worked with Dr Anuja Cabraal on this study.
2 I worked with Associate Professor Marg Liddell (RMIT University) and Dr Jasvinder Sidhu (Federation University Australia). We interviewed 30 women who had survived family violence (17 Indian and 13 Anglo-Celtic) and 17 persons from community organisations providing services related to family violence, and religious organisations.

Preface xiii

of the interviews were two hours long. With some, this was followed by a social visit, particularly if I was in the woman's home.

I recognised the interview offered a slice of the woman's experience of family violence and survival as she saw it at that time. Though the interview focused on money, gender and family violence, the open-ended interview often answered unasked questions.

I had informed consent from the women when I interviewed them for the research projects as part of the university ethics process. Recognising the story as told here would go into greater detail than any other kind of research writing, I sent the draft stories back to the participants to ensure they were comfortable with what I had written. One woman did not want her story told. She questioned why I hadn't told her I would be writing a book of stories when I first interviewed her and sought informed consent. I of course had not known at the time I would be writing this book. That is why I was going back to the women for consent.

Her withdrawal of consent hurt. I had not had such a withdrawal at the writing stage in 30 years of qualitative research. She of course had the right to withdraw. Her withdrawal also hurt because I admired her. Her story was a story of the trauma of family violence. It was an inspiring story of how a survivor of family violence had empowered herself through education and communication and was helping other women heal. We wished each other well, for both of us had the same aim of preventing and addressing family violence.

She left me and other qualitative researchers with two valuable suggestions. She said the informed consent form should be more explicit about the outputs. It should say a book may follow the research, rather than only saying the interview is 'for the purpose of research.' She also suggested I send an email to the woman saying I want to write her story, before surprising her with the draft. I agreed it was a more respectful way of proceeding. This is what I did with the last four stories. Three said yes. All the women reviewed the draft of their story to ensure it was true of their experience at the time of the interview.[3]

---

3   I have written of the ethics of writing of family violence in more detail in Singh, S. (2021). Telling Research: The Story of the Violence of Money. In the companion website to Richards, L. (2021). *Handling Qualitative Data: A Practical Guide* (4th edition), https://study.sagepub.com/richards4e/student-resources/telling-research/the-violence-of-money

The women found it difficult to tell their stories even though most were presently in a good place. Some of the women also found it difficult to read their own stories. It meant reliving the trauma. Hearing the stories was also traumatic. I had to seek professional counselling for the first time because of my research. But the stories were also empowering for they were stories of survival. The women had found themselves again and were able to look forward to a future they chose. They talked of family violence, money, and abuse with their children. Many of the women went on to help other women suffering family violence.

Through this book, their stories are told for researchers, practitioners, policy makers and victim-survivors. I hope the book leads to conversations about money in intimate relationships to help prevent the devastation of economic abuse.

1 Introduction
Economic abuse is the untold story of family violence

The silence around domestic economic abuse

Economic abuse is a part of the legal definition of family violence in Australia. However, family violence is still thought of as physical assault. The silence around economic abuse also reflects the difficulty of talking of money in intimate relationships. It can unravel issues of power, dependence and morality. '…Issues of power and control are closely intertwined with the negotiation of the balance between dependence and independence' (Finch & Mason, 1993, p. 58). Money is also seen as private, particularly in the 'mainstream' Anglo-Celtic community in Australia.[1] But this silence has contributed to 2.2 million women in Australia (Australian Bureau of Statistics [ABS], 2017a) experiencing the searing effects of family violence in silence and the perpetrators are not held to account.

The popular conception of family violence as physical assault is supported by the fact that only the physical assault component of family violence is directly criminalised in Australia. The exception is Tasmania where economic and emotional abuse has been a crime since 2005. But even in Tasmania there is little public awareness of economic abuse. Kerryne Barwick who has prosecuted family violence cases in Tasmania notes a woman will report abuse only when there is physical assault. It is the prosecutor who may discover there is a long history of economic abuse (Barwick, 2017).

I am a sociologist of money, but it was only through my research on economic abuse that I recognised I too am a survivor. Reading the

---

1 The ancestry of the Anglo-Celtic group in Australia is predominantly English, Irish, and Scottish (Australian Bureau of Statistics, 1995). This is the dominant community in Australia, accounting for at least 39 per cent of the population in 2016 (Australian Bureau of Statistics, 2018).

DOI: 10.4324/9781003178606-1

Introduction

2016 report of the State of Victoria Royal Commission into Family Violence (State of Victoria Royal Commission into Family Violence, 2014–2016), I read that gambling is an example of economic abuse, and my first husband gambled.

Economic abuse is difficult to anticipate or recognise. I am a writer and academic with a graduate education from India, the United States and Australia. Like the women in these stories, I was used to financial independence before marriage. I did not anticipate that migration and young children would restrict my employment options, making me financially dependent on my husband for a few years. Like most people, I did not see my lack of access to money as economic abuse or family violence.

I did not make a submission to the State of Victoria Royal Commission into Family Violence (2016), for I had studied money as a medium of care rather than abuse. I was not alone. There is not a single reference to the sociology of money in the eight-volume final report of the Royal Commission. As sociologists of money, we have been remiss in not going deeper into issues around power and domination in intimate relationships.

Sociologists of money have mainly studied the control of money in the household and family as reflected in decision making. The study of money in the family has also focussed on how power, gender inequality and ideologies of marriage influence the agenda for decision making (Nyman, 2003; Vogler, 1998). These approaches reflect the one-dimensional and two-dimensional versions of power, focussing on overt and covert conflict (Lukes, 2005). We have not yet studied how money in the family connects to domination that is 'power *over* another'. This third dimension is closely related to 'subordination, subjugation, control, conformism, acquiescence and docility' (p. 74). Therefore sociologists of money, other than Jan Pahl in her early work (Pahl, 1985), have had little influence on how we have thought of, or talked about the violence of money.

Domestic economic abuse and its prevalence

The 12 stories in this book are of Anglo-Celtic and Indian women in Australia who suffered and survived economic abuse. They describe a range of actions that count as abuse: a husband denies his wife money; monitors what she spends; spends the money in the household on himself; fails to provide; pushes the wife to earn and then appropriates her earnings; saddles her with debt; demands dowry; sends all his earnings and some of hers to his parents; sabotages her work; destroys her mobile phone and contacts, appropriates her savings and property;

drags her through court processes to impoverish her and the children; and does not pay child support.

These actions during the marriage and after separation, cover the three areas of economic abuse: economic control, economic exploitation, and employment sabotage (Postmus, Hoge, Breckenridge, Sharp-Jeffs, & Chung, 2018). 'Economic abuse' and 'financial abuse' are often used interchangeably because money is central to both. However, economic abuse is a broader concept for it involves coercive control of money as well as other economic resources, such as the use of a car, a place to live, communications devices, and enabling oneself to engage in paid work through enhancing language and skills and obtaining appropriate registration of qualifications (Adams, Sullivan, Bybee, & Greeson, 2008; Sharp-Jeffs & Learmonth, 2017).

We do not have reliable estimates of the prevalence of economic abuse in Australia. The estimated proportion of women who have suffered economic abuse range widely depending on how economic abuse is measured. The Australian Bureau of Statistics' latest *Personal Safety Survey, 2016*, has not separately measured economic abuse. It includes six questions relating to economic abuse as part of the 20 questions on emotional abuse by a current or previous cohabiting partner since the age of 15. This is repeated economic abuse to control or harm the person (Australian Bureau of Statistics [ABS], 2017b). Another Australian study estimated the lifetime prevalence of economic abuse to be 11.5 per cent overall, with 15.7 per cent of Australian women and 7.1 per cent for men (Kutin, Russell, & Reid, 2017). Studies in the United States and the United Kingdom put the prevalence of economic abuse at 40–99 per cent of women who have suffered intimate partner violence (IPV) (Adams et al., 2008; Postmus, Plummer, McMahon, Murshid, & Kim, 2012; Sharp-Jeffs, 2015).

We can say even less about economic abuse among culturally and linguistically diverse (CALD) women in Australia. They are usually not adequately represented in surveys because of difficulties of language, at times a cultural acceptance of family violence, and difficulties of sharing the experience with outsiders. We do know that women migrants with weak networks in Australia and an incomplete understanding of the support available will less often seek help. When they do, they do not know whether they will be heard through a cultural lens of money other than their own (Mitra-Kahn, Newbigin, & Hardefeldt, 2016; Vaughan et al., 2016).

Most women experience economic abuse together with physical, emotional, and/or sexual abuse (Sharp-Jeffs & Learmonth, 2017). Stylianou, Postmus and McMahon (2013) drew on a study in the

4 *Introduction*

United States to note that 76 per cent of the women who experienced physical and/or psychological abuse also suffered economic abuse. Similarly, research by Adams et al. (2008) concluded that 'economic abuse is a significant component of the broad system of tactics used by abusive men to gain power and maintain control over their partners' (Adams et al., 2008, p. 580).

There are robust debates around gender and family violence. Early quantitative studies in the United States showed that men and women were nearly equally violent in marriage, though men's violence was more injurious (Straus, Gelles, & Steinmetz, 1980). However, feminist studies of battered wives in the United States and United Kingdom showed it was women who predominantly suffered family violence (Dobash & Dobash, 1979). Michael Johnson made sense of these conflicting figures by distinguishing between 'situational couple violence,' 'intimate terrorism', and 'violent resistance' (Johnson, 2008). Situational couple violence deals with occasional conflict that escalates to violence. It is not about general control. It is this kind of violence that Straus and his colleagues measured. Intimate terrorism that is rooted in male control and patriarchy is wholly perpetrated by men. Violent resistance is by women striking back after years of brutal violence by their husbands.

The Australian Bureau of Statistics finds, 'Approximately one in four women (23 per cent or 2.2 million) experienced violence by an intimate partner, compared to one in thirteen men (7.8 per cent or 703,700)' (Australian Bureau of Statistics [ABS], 2017a).[2] The intimate partner homicide figures show that it is women who are the victims of IPV. They have been subject to intimate terrorism or have shown violent resistance to abuse. In New South Wales (NSW), 80 per cent (234) of intimate partner homicide victims between 2017 and 2019 were women. Most of the 20 per cent (58) of men were killed by women (51) and men (7) they abused (NSW Domestic Violence Death Review Team, 2020).

Feminist scholars and activists have described family violence as being rooted in patriarchal domination. 'The problem lies in the domination of women' (Dobash & Dobash, 1979, p. 243). Economic abuse, like other elements of family violence, increases with gender inequality in a society (Our Watch, Australia's National Research Organisation for Women's Safety [ANROWS], & VicHealth, 2015). The Victorian Royal Commission into Family Violence concluded:

---

2 This figure refers to the assault or threat of physical and sexual violence by a current or previous cohabiting partner and current or previous boyfriend/girlfriend/date.

The causes of family violence are complex and include gender inequality and community attitudes towards women. Contributing factors may include financial pressures, alcohol and drug abuse, mental illness and social and economic exclusion' (State of Victoria Royal Commission into Family Violence, 2016, p. 2).

As the women's stories will show, economic abuse makes it particularly difficult for a woman to leave the home and marriage. Across cultures, women who become economically dependent on their partner are less likely to leave abusive relationships, fearing homelessness and not being able to provide for themselves and their children (Adams et al., 2008; Australia's National Research Organisation for Women's Safety, 2019; Postmus, Plummer, & Stylianou, 2016; Sharp-Jeffs & Learmonth, 2017). At times, women covertly prepare to leave by trying to gain more education, hiding money or assets, while making sure they have access to relevant financial documents (Llyod, 1997; Sanders, 2015). When women do leave, they often have coerced debt, that is, 'all nonconsensual, credit-related transactions that occur in a violent relationship' (Littwin, 2012, p. 954).

Migrant women find it more difficult to leave. Poverty, low socioeconomic status and belonging to a cultural, racial or ethnic minority increase the difficulties of survivors trying to achieve economic independence (Peled & Krigel, 2016). The impediments increase if the women do not have fluency in English. Few family violence services have bilingual and bi-cultural staff. Conditions attached to temporary non-partner visas restrict their access to help with housing, finance and health services. Moreover, these women and others with temporary partner visas are often threatened by their partner and/or his family that if they do not comply with their wishes, they will be deported. The women often do not know that for temporary partner visas, there are provisions in the Migration Act for the woman to obtain permanent residence if she can show evidence of family violence (Koleth, Serova, & Trojanowska, 2020; Segrave, 2017).

Economic abuse can continue long after separation with perpetrators using fragmented legal systems, the high costs of extended legal processes and withholding child support to keep their ex-partners and children in poverty (Camilleri et al., 2015; Douglas, 2018; Fehlberg and Millward, 2014; Macdonald, 2012; Smallwood, 2015; State of Victoria, 2016, Surviving Economic Abuse & Standard Life Foundation, 2021).

Family violence has devastating consequences. It leads to the decimation of self-confidence, mental and physical health problems, and continued financial insecurity for women and their children (Alhabib et al., 2010; Bevin, 2016; Cameron, 2014; McMahon and McGorrery, 2016; Pollett, 2011; Postmus et al., 2012b; Sharp-Jeffs, 2015; Sharp, 2008; Smallwood, 2015; State of Victoria, 2016; Vaughan et al., 2016; VicHealth, 2014). Poverty associated with economic abuse significantly predicts these adverse health impacts.

A US study of mothers found that economic abuse is more predictive of depression than psychological or physical abuse (Postmus et al., 2012a). Webster studying emotional abuse (Webster, 2016) says IPV is the single largest predictor of mental and physical ill-health for Australian women aged 18–44 years. IPV is a greater risk than 'tobacco use, high cholesterol or use of illicit drugs' (p. 7). It leads to poor mental health and problems during pregnancy and birth, alcohol and illicit drug use, suicide and homicide.

Despite the grievous impact of economic abuse and other non-physical dimensions of family violence, the police, prosecutors, judges, and victim-survivors themselves in Australia continue to emphasise physical assault as family violence. This is against the finding that intimate partner homicides related to family violence are nearly always preceded by coercive and controlling behaviour (NSW Domestic Violence Death Review Team, 2020). The earlier review by this team in 2017 found that using physical abuse as the sole predictor for domestic violence related homicide would have missed 11 of the 77 cases reviewed. The Domestic Violence Death Review Team has recommended that greater emphasis be laid on coercive and controlling behaviour.

Coercive control is at the centre of family violence

Coercive control is at the centre of most economic abuse as well as other dimensions of family violence. It is a gendered pattern of behaviour designed to entrap a woman through isolation, fear and intimidation, to take away her freedom and human rights.

The concept of coercive control has been getting more media attention in Australia in 2020 and 2021. In February 2020, Hannah Clarke and her three children were burnt to death by her estranged husband. Hannah Clarke had not been physically assaulted but had suffered coercive control during her marriage. This has sparked calls for criminalising coercive control in 2020. It is a new concept for most. None of the women whose stories are told in this book, spoke of their experience in 2016 and 2017 in terms of coercive control. The women spoke of isolation, control, and living in constant fear of abuse. They talked of 'walking on eggshells,' not knowing when their husbands would erupt. Some spoke of slavery and torture. The longer they stayed, the more they wondered whether they were to blame. Some feared they were losing their mind. They did not know that their stories are stories of coercive control.

Evan Stark, the most influential writer on coercive control (Stark, 2009, 2012, 2020; Stark & Hester, 2019) describes family violence as a malevolent pattern of behaviour. It is not a one-off episode where a person has lost control. It is continuous and routine, a thought-out pattern of behaviour with strategic intent. He argues that coercive control is 'used to hurt and intimidate victims (coercion) and ...designed to isolate and regulate them (control).' (2012, p. 207). He defines the tactics of coercive control as gendered. They include:

> ... forms of constraint and the monitoring and/or regulation of commonplace activities of daily living, particularly those associated with women's default roles as mothers, homemakers, and sexual partners, and run the gamut from their access to money, food, and transport to how they dress, clean, cook, or perform sexually. (Stark, 2012, p. 201)

Coercive control is gendered as it is predominantly rooted in patriarchy and men's sense of entitlement and privilege. It also works through the man's interpretation of gendered stereotypes to accuse the woman that she is not a good mother, wife, cook, housewife, or lover. He tells her she is unattractive and does not know how to manage money. Coercive control is the strategy that men use to preserve their entitlements. The man, with malicious intent, isolates her from her family and friends so that in time she can only see his version of her. She begins to feel his violence is her fault, that she has brought the violence on herself. He dominates and entraps a woman through fear into doing what he directs. He uses surveillance, micromanages her daily life through 'rules,' withholding food, communication and money, degradation, the use of shaming tactics and threats to the safety of children. This control increases with time as the woman learns to fear the consequences of not obeying her husband (Stark, 2009, 2012).

Coercive control is a narrative of behaviour over time. It has three thresholds. The first stage of grooming comprises courtship, fear, emotional abuse and isolation. The second is coercive behaviour. This involves pervasive demands, credible threats and surveillance. The third threshold is the victim's response where there is fear, instability, an elusive sense of personal control and personality change (Wiener, 2017). Wiener was writing of these thresholds so that the police could make sense of coercive control. But these thresholds are also evident in the stories of the women that follow.

This narrative of coercive control differs from the prevalent 'violent incident model,' where violent incidents can be given a time and date, supported by evidence of cuts, bruises and hospital visits. Cassandra Wiener discussing the criminalisation of coercive control that came into force in England and Wales in December 2015, writes of a policewoman investigating domestic rape, who heard the woman telling her story of abuse. Noticing a dog bowl on the floor, the policewoman asked the woman why she has a dog bowl when she does not have a dog. The woman told her that was where she had her supper. If she didn't, the alternatives were worse (Wiener, 2017).

The women's stories show that control over the mobile phone, computers, the Internet and the car has increasingly become part of the way a man isolates, monitors and abuses a woman. The technologies that are generally seen as ways of connecting, become technology-facilitated abuse in family violence. They are used for isolating a woman, attacking her privacy, placing her under constant surveillance, stalking, stealing identity, image-based abuse, and fake social media accounts. This is true within an intimate relationship and it can continue after the relationship ends (Australian Government eSafety Commissioner, Not dated; Dragiewicz et al., 2919; Maher, McCulloch, & Fitz-Gibbon, 2017; Powell & Henry, 2017; Segrave & Vitis, 2017).

There is a debate around criminalising coercive control in Australia. Much of the discussion revolves around issues of law, policing and prosecution. But at the centre is a major issue of social change that is the criminalisation of the non-physical dimensions of family violence. Emotional and economic abuse can then be seen as a crime, which has consequences for the perpetrators. The law will have a symbolic and educative role in increasing recognition of economic abuse as family violence. This change rivals the major social change when family violence became a social law and order issue, rather than a private conflict behind closed doors.

As indicated earlier, England and Wales legislated to criminalise coercive and controlling behaviour at the end of December 2015. Scotland and Ireland introduced new laws in 2018. Preliminary data on how the law in England and Wales (2015) has worked, shows that policing and prosecution have taken into account the gendered nature of coercive control with men predominantly being the perpetrators. The new law has changed media reporting of family violence with a greater understanding of coercive control as domination and entrapment. The imbalance of power in intimate relationships is now better recognised in court decisions. The cases prosecuted under the 2015 England and Wales law on coercive control have been extreme cases of coercive control that were morally and legally indefensible. Men have pleaded guilty at a higher rate than usual. However, problems remain with training and under prosecuting (McGorrery & McMahon, 2019; Tolmie, 2018; Wangmann, 2020; Wiener, 2020).

Criminalising coercive control faces challenges of training and mind set. Police need to gather evidence of coercive control rather than just document incidents of physical violence A focus on coercive control changes what is 'seen' and 'heard' by the police and the courts (Stark, 2020). However, the changes required of the legal system were even more dramatic when family violence laws were first introduced (Dobash & Dobash, 1992).

The legal discussions in Australia revolve around whether a new law will remedy the 'gap' in the criminalisation of family violence or whether existing laws like those relating to 'torture' in Queensland can address coercive control. Is the system too blunt to move away from an incident-based model to recognise and prosecute ongoing and continuous controlling and coercive behaviour? The fear is the new law may succeed in downplaying physical violence, while failing those it seeks to protect (Bishop & Bettinson, 2018; Burman & Brooks-Hay, 2018; Douglas, 2020; McMahon & McGorrery, 2020; Neave, 2020; Quilter, 2020; Tolmie, 2018; Walklate & Fitz-Gibbon, 2019; Wangmann, 2020; Wiener, 2017, 2020).

These legal discussions do not change the importance of such a law to signal social change in criminalising economic and emotional abuse. It is important however, for the new law to address some important questions around framing the criminalisation of coercive control. Tolmie (2018) asks: How can coercive control be identified when male dominance in everyday life involves a measure of 'unpaid servitude' by women? (p. 56) Where should the line be drawn between normal and abusive behaviour that exploits existing gender norms? (Tolmie, 2018; Tuerkheimer, 2004). NSW State Parliament's inquiry into criminalising coercive control translates this question to economic abuse and asks: How can we demarcate coercive and controlling behaviours on the one hand and voluntary choices in a relationship on the other hand? For instance, when one person controls money in the household, it may indicate coercive control or it may signal a consensual arrangement in an intimate relationship (NSW Government, 2020, p. 8).

The women's stories in this book also prompt other questions that have yet to be asked about coercive control in multicultural societies. How will the new law 'cloak' the experience of coercive control in extended families which can be the norm in the global South? How do we prevent branding culturally accepted control in another society as abusive, while seeing it as reasonable in our own? The 'reasonable person' who represents a particular socio-demographic and cultural perspective is part of Scottish and Irish legislation and implied in the Tasmanian legislation (Wangmann, 2020).

To prevent seeing coercive control only in 'other' cultures, policy makers and practitioners need to turn to the sociology of money to understand how the gender and morality of money shape the medium of economic abuse across generations and cultures.

The gender and morality of money across cultures

The women's stories show the nature of economic abuse and coercive control is the same across cultures and generations. The impact of economic abuse is always devastating but the medium of economic abuse differs. Some women experience economic abuse through the misuse of the joint account, others through a separate account, or temporarily no account at all. Coercive control is not something that resides in a particular cultural practice of money.

For some women, it is the husband who is the perpetrator. For other women living in a joint or extended family, the husband can be aided by his parents and siblings.

To understand the gender and morality of money, it is essential to understand that money has different social and cultural meanings across cultures. Viviana Zelizer has written profoundly about how money shapes and is shaped by social relationships and cultural values. There are different kinds of monies which are intersected with morals, emotions and power. Money is earmarked based on its moral and social meanings, source and use. People engage in relational work, trying to match moral frameworks, relationships and communication with appropriate economic transactions (Bandelj, et al., 2017; Bandelj, Wherry, & Zelizer, 2017; Wherry, 2016, 2017; Zelizer, 1994, 2005, 2012).

Women and men own, inherit, manage and control money differently in the household and family across cultures. The 'gender of money' differs across and within cultures over generations, reflecting the ideology of marriage and cohabitation, kinship norms, household and family formation, socioeconomic differences, and the legal and religious status of women. It changes across life stage when couples have children, get unemployed or retire.

Jan Pahl set the conceptual frameworks of how money is managed and controlled by women and men in a nuclear household. It varies from the wife managing the money while the husband controls it, to levels of partial or full jointness or independent control and management where the husband and wife manage and control their own money (Pahl, 1989, 2008; Vogler & Pahl, 1993). Together with Mala Bhandari, I built on Pahl's work to study money in the three or four generational Indian joint family in urban middle-income families. Management and control of money was dominantly male but could differ across generations within the same family (Singh & Bhandari, 2012).

The gender of money is legitimised by the moral norms associated with how 'good' parents, children, husbands and wives are defined. Morality, religion and law often intertwine. These values are buttressed by third party valuations of whether the morality of money is in tune with the decisions and transactions of money. The moral power of money positions a person in the hierarchies of family, religion, politics and finance (Wherry, 2016; Wilkis, 2018; Zelizer, 1985, 2011a). This is illustrated poignantly by Akuei (2005) describing a Dinka man from South Sudan, resettled in the West, trying to accommodate family and lineage demands for remittances against his limited income and settlement expenses. It was important for him to meet these obligations so that he himself and others in his family and lineage thought of him as 'a good moral person' (p. 4).

The different moralities of money across culture struck me when I was researching money in Anglo-Celtic marriage in the early 1990s. I was interviewing an older woman in her Housing Commission unit. I had earlier interviewed her son in his lovely home with a swimming pool in a different suburb. I asked his mother whether her son helped her financially. This question came from the moral norms around money in India where children are expected to show filial care through money. I sent money home to my mother when I became financially resilient. But the woman said she did not expect her son to contribute, for he had his own financial responsibilities. She also said she did not want it, for she was able to manage.

I was struck by this difference. My mother was also able to manage but she boasted about the money she received because it demonstrated she had raised a filial child. I worried whether my 20-year-old son would imbibe these norms in Australia and lack the values around money and family that I considered moral. I came home and told him that when he grew up and wanted to give me money, I would be delighted to receive it.

I also came back thinking this woman's son was uncaring. Later, I realised he had shown care, but not through money. He took his mother shopping, drove her to the doctor, cleaned the gutters, mowed the grass, maintained, or renovated her home. Doing things for his mother was his medium of care.

This interview starkly laid out that in Anglo-Celtic culture, money goes one way from grandparents to grandchildren, from parents to children. This one-way flow is partly because Australia has a social welfare protective net. It is also because gifting money has not always been acceptable. In the 1990s a grandmother could put $20[3] inside a birthday card for her grandchild. However, money was not the preferred gift as at an Indian marriage, birth, or festival.

But the gender and morality of money changes across generations. It was transformed for middle-income Anglo-Celtic married couples in the 1950s as more women went into paid work. In my research on money and Anglo-Celtic marriage, most women who had married in the 1960s had joint bank accounts. They saw their marriage as a partnership. But they remembered their mothers often received a housekeeping allowance. The father was the provider, the mother the home maker, particularly when the children were young (Singh, 1997).

Money traditionally has been male in India. Men across generations most often control the money in the three generational patrilineal joint family. The joint family is the normative idea of family in India, where a son brings his wife to stay with his parents, and in time their children grow up in the paternal grandparents' house. The maleness of money continues in India. But middle-income women, particularly in large cities, are more likely to be in paid work, compared with their parents. Legal and social entitlements for women have increased.

Migration influences changes in the gender of money. When a man or woman migrates alone to support the family in the home country, the migrant controls the sending of money, but may have little influence on its use. These changes may revert to the traditional pattern when the migrant returns (Gamburd, 1998; Kurien, 2002; Parreñas, 2005; Rahman, 2008). When a woman migrates with her husband and children, she may become the main earner with or without a change in the gender of money (George, 2005).

Most of the Indian women in the stories that follow were in paid work and often the main earners, whereas their fathers had been the main earners. In the Indian community in Australia, older women told how they signed off their inheritance to their brothers, but they themselves intended to leave their property equally to their sons and

---

3 The money is in Australian dollars

Introduction 13

daughters. Sons were traditionally charged with the care of their parents. But migration and changes in the gender of education and professional earnings have meant it can be just as important to have a 'good daughter' as a 'filial son' (Singh, 2016).

As the stories will show, these changes in the gender and morality of money are uneven, with old and new norms coexisting awkwardly. Anglo-Celtic women can still see the husband as the provider as in previous generations while jointness and togetherness are currently the central tenets of Anglo-Celtic marriage. Holding on to conflicting norms also explains why some young urban professional women in the Indian community in Australia with greater autonomy can be comfortable depositing their money in their husband's account, trusting he will look after their welfare. Among Indian married women in Australia today, there is a greater realisation that a son's duty towards his parents in the source country has to be balanced against the settlement needs of his nuclear family in Australia. Moreover, moral norms relating to a 'good daughter' are entering discussions when it comes to sending money home (Singh, 2016, 2019).

The direction and range of moral obligations tie in with the way money and family are defined and perceived. Among middle-income Anglo-Celtic couples in Australia the couple is the financial unit. Joint bank accounts are held by the couple, rather than parents and children, or siblings. Money is private to the couple. The couple will most often not discuss their money with adult children or their parents. There have been changes recently as parents have given or lent their adult children money, as housing prices have risen. One study revealed that more than one-third of a sample of 7000 Australians, 50 years and over, have informally lent or gifted money to their adult children (Olsberg & Winters, 2005). But money most often still goes one way down the generations.

In India the family, nuclear or extended, is the private boundary around money. Money travels two-ways between generations. Joint bank accounts may be held by the couple, but often also are between parents and children and among siblings. Joint accounts, where they exist, do not symbolise marriage. Joint accounts enable protection, for in the most common 'either or' joint bank account in India, the money goes to the survivor outside the estate (Singh, 2009).

In India as well as the global South, which includes Asia, the Pacific, Africa, the Middle East and Latin America, money is a preferred gift to mark life events, such as birth, marriage and death. Money is also an important medium of care. In India, parents feel it is moral to give money in a timely manner to their adult children, particularly the sons. Traditionally, it is also a son's duty to send money to his parents. Parents accept this money from children, for it is evidence they have filial children (Singh, 2016; Singh & Bhandari, 2012). In some parts of the global South, depending on a person's recognised boundary of family, the migrant may send money home to parents and the nuclear family or also include a wider group of extended kin of both the husband and wife (Akuei, 2005; Lindley, 2009).

The melding of the morality of money in the family and funds transfer has led to formal international remittances – money sent by migrants to their parents and other family left behind – becoming one of the largest international transfer of funds. International remittances that flow through financial institutions and mobile money are larger than foreign direct investment (FDI), and official development assistance (ODA) to low and middle-income countries (LMICs). This excludes China. Even during 2020 when the COVID-19 pandemic continued to spread, remittances to LMICs defied predictions of a deep slide. They proved resilient at US$540 billion, with only a slight drop of 1.6 per cent compared to the year before. India received the highest remittances in 2020 at US$83 billion. It was followed by China, Mexico, the Philippines and Egypt (Ratha et al., 2021).

There are several 'scripts' for remittances, ranging from compensation to donations (Carling, 2014). Most often money goes from the migrant to the family left behind. However, in middle and high-income countries, money can flow from the source country to the migrant. Parents give money to their adult children to help with education and settlement expenses. Most of the Indian international students in Australia are funded by their parents selling stocks and/or property, or emptying their savings and retirement funds. It is seen as moral to give when it is most needed, assuming that the children will also be filial and help their parents as they age (Singh & Cabraal, 2014; Singh & Gatina, 2015).

Money is culturally shaped, but the common thread of the gender of money across cultures is that men have usually been the main earners and/or own the most productive resources. As money earned is often seen as money owned, these higher earnings give men a sense of entitlement over money. Yet when women have financial choices, they spend more of their money on the household and children compared to men. This 'selfless spending becomes a hallmark of moral virtue' (Zelizer, 2011b). Mary Ellen Iskenderian, President and CEO of Women's World Banking said in 2017, 'On average, women spend 90 cents out of every dollar earned on education, health care and housing, in comparison to men's 60 cents' (Iskenderian, 2017).

Writing the stories

The stories of 12 Anglo-Celtic and Indian women that follow, draw on open-ended interviews I conducted between May 2016 and September 2017. These interviews were wholly in English, or in a mixture of English, Punjabi, and Hindi. Most of the women had professional and/or graduate education and were often in paid work. Six of the 12 were the main earners in the household.

The women chose where they wanted to be interviewed, so it was either in their home, or in my office. One chose her place of work. Each interview lasted for about two hours with the associated visit component going further. In two cases, I was with the woman and her family for four hours. The interviews focussed on understanding the woman's experience and survival of family violence with an emphasis on economic abuse.

The stories were difficult to tell and hear. Even when the family violence took place two decades ago, the experience seemed present in the telling of their stories. For four of the 12 women, economic abuse continued after separation and divorce. They told their stories because they wanted to share the devastation of family violence and what they had learned.

These stories give the lived experience of the violence of money in intimate relationships across cultures. They illustrate the silence around domestic economic abuse and how women did not see this abuse as family violence. The stories show how in different ways, the husbands have denied money to their wives by not providing, emptied the joint accounts, questioned even $2 they spent, appropriated their assets, and sabotaged their attempts to engage in paid work. In Indian joint families, the husband's family sometimes aided or initiated the abuse.

Economic abuse was always emotionally abusive. At times, it was accompanied by physical violence and in one story, reproductive violence. The women were isolated, sometimes even denied mobile phones and the Internet. They lived in fear, not knowing when and how the violence would descend on them. They suffered mental and physical ill-health, and lost confidence in themselves. They were denied freedom and there were times when they felt they were losing their mind.

They survived. They spoke of the terrible experience of family violence, but for most, it was past. A few continue to struggle towards financial resilience. At the end of one interview with a woman who had experienced 20 years of economic abuse, I commented that she had survived. She hugged me and said, 'Not survived Supriya, empowered.'

References

Adams, A. E., Sullivan, C. M., Bybee, D., & Greeson, M. R. (2008). Development of the scale of economic abuse. *Violence Against Women, 14*(5), 563–588. Retrieved from http://vaw.sagepub.com/content/14/5/563.long

Akuei, S. R. (2005). *Remittances as Unforeseen Burdens: The Livelihoods and Social Obligations of Sudanese Refugees*. Retrieved from Geneva: https://www.csrf-southsudan.org/repository/remittances-unforesseen-burdens-livelihoods-social-obligations-sudanes-refugees/

Alhabib, S., Nur, U., & Jones, R. (2010). Domestic violence against women: Systematic review of prevalence studies. *Journal of Family Violence, 25*(4), 369–382. doi: 10.1007/s10896-009-9298-4

Australia's National Research Organisation for Women's Safety (ANROWS). (2019). *Domestic and Family Violence, Housing Insecurity and Homelessness: Research Synthesis*. Retrieved from Sydney: https://20ian81kynqg38bl3l3eh8bf-wpengine.netdna-ssl.com/wp-content/uploads/2019/03/DV-Housing-Homelessness-Synthesis-2.Ed_.pdf

Australian Bureau of Statistics (ABS). (1995). *1301.0 - Year Book Australia, 1995: Ethnic and Cultural Diversity in Australia*. Retrieved from Canberra: http://www.abs.gov.au/Ausstats/abs@.nsf/94713ad445ff1425ca25682000192af2/49f609c-83cf34d69ca2569de0025c182!OpenDocument

Australian Bureau of Statistics (ABS). (2017a). *4906.0 - Personal Safety, Australia, 2016*. Retrieved from Canberra: http://www.abs.gov.au/ausstats/abs@.nsf/mf/4906.0

Australian Bureau of Statistics (ABS). (2017b). *Personal Safety Survey, Australia: User Guide, 2016*. Retrieved from Canberra: https://www.abs.gov.au/ausstats/abs@.nsf/Lookup/4906.0.55.003main+features202016

Australian Bureau of Statistics (ABS). (2018). *2016 Census QuickStats*. Retrieved from Canberra: http://quickstats.censusdata.abs.gov.au/census_services/getproduct/census/2016/quickstat/036?opendocument

Australian Government eSafety Commissioner. (Not dated). *Domestic and Family Violence*. Retrieved from https://www.esafety.gov.au/key-issues/domestic-family-violence

Bandelj, N., Boston, T., Elyachar, J., Kim, J., McBride, M., Tufail, Z., & Weatherall, J. O. (2017). Morals and emotions of money. In N. Bandelj, F. F. Wherry, & V. A. Zelizer (Eds.), *Money Talks: Explaining How Money Really Works* (pp. 39–56). Princeton: Princeton University Press.

Bandelj, N., Wherry, F. F., & Zelizer, V. A. (Eds.). (2017). *Money Talks: Explaining How Money Really Works*. Princeton and Oxford: Princeton University Press.

Barwick, K. (2017). Emotional Abuse, Intimidation and Economic Abuse in Tasmania. Unpublished.

Bevin, E. (2016, 1 Aug). *Tasmanian man accused of preventing wife from making decisions, accessing joint accounts*. Retrieved from http://www.abc.net.au/news/2016-08-01/tasmanian-man-prosecuted-for-alleged-economic-abuse/7679922

Bishop, C., & Bettinson, V. (2018). Evidencing domestic violence, including behaviour that falls under the new offence of 'controlling and coercive behaviour.' *International Journal of Evidence & Proof*, 22(1), 3–29. Retrieved from https://journals.sagepub.com/doi/full/10.1177/1365712717725535

Burman, M., & Brooks-Hay, O. (2018). Aligning policy and law? The creation of a domestic abuse offence incorporating coercive control. *Criminology & Criminal Justice*, 18(1), 67–83. Retrieved from https://doi.org/10.1177/1748895817752223

Cameron, P. (2014). *Relationship Problems and Money: Women Talk about Financial Abuse*. Retrieved from West Melbourne: http://www.wire.org.au/wp-content/uploads/2014/08/WIRE-Research-Report_Relationship-Problems-and-Money-Women-talk-about-financial-abuse-August2014 accessed 4 May 2014

Camilleri, O., Corrie, T., & Moore, S. (2015). *Restoring Financial Safety: Legal Responses to Economic Abuse*. Retrieved from Melbourne: https://www.westjustice.org.au/cms_uploads/docs/westjustice-restoring-financial-safety-report.pdf#:~:text=Restoring%20Financial%20Safety%3A%20Legal%20responses%20to%20economic%20abuse,them%20with%20better%20services%20to%20help%20them%20recover.

Carling, J. (2014). Scripting remittances: Making sense of money transfers in transnational relationships. *International Migration Review*, 48, S218–S262. doi:10.1111/imre.12143

Dobash, R. E., & Dobash, R. (1979). *Violence Against Wives: A Case Against the Patriarchy*. New York: The Free Press.

Dobash, R. E., & Dobash, R. P. (1992). *Women, Violence and Social Change*. London and New York: Routledge.

Douglas, H. (2018). Legal systems abuse and coercive control. *Criminology & Criminal Justice*, 18(1), 84–99.

Douglas, H. (2020). Alternative constructions of a family violence offence. In M. McMahon, & P. McGorrery (Eds.), *Criminalising Family Violence: Family Violence and the Criminal Law* (pp. 243–260). Singapore: Springer Nature Singapore Pte Ltd.

Dragiewicz, M., Harris, B., Woodlock, D., Salter, M., Easton, H., Lynch, A., Campbell, H., Leach, J., & Milne, L. (2019). *Domestic Violence and Communication Technology: Survivor Experiences of Intrusion, Surveillance, and Identity Crime*. Retrieved from Sydney: https://accan.org.au/Domestic%20Violence%20and%20Communication%20Technology%20final%20report%2020190801.pdf

Fehlberg, B., & Millward, C. (2014). Family violence and financial outcomes after parental separation. In A. Hayes & D. Higgins (Eds.), *Families, Policy and the Law: Selected Essays on Contemporary Issues for Australia* (pp. 235–243). Melbourne: Australian Institute of Family Studies.

Finch, J., & Mason, J. (1993). *Negotiating Family Responsibilities*. London: Routledge.

Gamburd, M. R. (1998). Absent women and their extended families: Sri Lanka's migrant housemaids. In C. Risseeuw, & K. Ganesh (Eds.), *Negotiation and Social Space: A Gendered Analysis of Changing Kin and Security Networks in South Asia and Sub-Saharan Africa* (pp. 276–291). Walnut Creek, CA: AltaMira Press.

George, S. M. (2005). *When Women Come First: Gender and Class in Transnational Migration*. Berkeley: University of California Press.

Iskenderian, M. E. (2017, 12 July). Beyond microfinance: Empowering women in the developing world. *House Committee on Foreign Affairs*. Retrieved from http://docs.house.gov/meetings/FA/FA00/20170712/106233/HHRG-115-FA00-Wstate-IskenderianM-20170712.pdf

Johnson, M. P.(2008). *A Typology of Domestic Violence: Intimate Terrorism, Violent Resistance, and Situational Couple Violence*. Boston: Northeastern University Press.

Koleth, M., Serova, N., & Trojanowska, B. K. (2020). *Prevention and Safer Pathways to Services for Migrant and Refugee Communities: Ten Research Insights from the Culturally and Linguistically Diverse Projects with Action Research (CALD PAR) Initiative*. Retrieved from Sydney, NSW: https://d2rn9gno7zhxqg.cloudfront.net/wp-content/uploads/2020/04/21093608/ANROWS_CALD_PAR_Summary_report20.1.pdf

Kurien, P. A. (2002). *Kaleidoscopic Ethnicity: International Migration and the Reconstruction of Community Identities in India*. New Delhi: Oxford University Press.

Kutin, J., Russell, R., & Reid, M. (2017). Economic abuse between intimate partners in Australia: Prevalence, health status, disability and financial stress. *Australian and New Zealand Journal of Public Health, 14*(3), 269–274. doi:10.1111/1753-6405.12651

Lindley, A. (2009). The early-morning phonecall: Remittances from a refugee diaspora perspective. *Journal of Ethnic and Migration Studies, 35*(8), 1315–1334. Retrieved from http://www.informaworld.com/10.1080/13691830903123112

Littwin, A. (2012). Coerced debt: The role of consumer credit in domestic violence. *California Law Review, 100*(4), 951–1025. Retrieved from https://scholarship.law.berkeley.edu/cgi/viewcontent.cgi?article=4178&context=californialawreview

Lloyd, S. (1997). The effects of domestic violence on women's employment. *Law & Policy, 19*(2), 139–167.

Lukes, S. (2005). *Power: A Radical View* (Second ed.). New York: Macmillan.

Macdonald, F. (2012). *Spotlight on Economic Abuse: a Literature and Policy Review*. Melbourne: Good Shepherd Youth & Family Service and Kildonan UnitingCare.

Maher, J., McCulloch, J., & Fitz-Gibbon, K. (2017). New forms of gendered surveillance? Intersections of technology and family violence. In M. Segrave, & L. Vitis (Eds.), *Gender, Technology and Violence* (pp. 38–53). Abingdon, Oxon and New York: Routledge.

McGorrery, P., & McMahon, M. (2019). Prosecuting controlling or coercive behaviour in England and Wales: Media reports of a novel offence. *Criminology & Criminal Justice*, 1–19. doi:10.1177/1748895819880947

McMahon, M., & McGorrery, P. (2016). Criminalising controlling and coercive behaviour: The next step in the prosecution of family violence? *Alternative Law Journal*, 41(2), 98–101.

McMahon, M., & McGorrery, P. (2020). Criminalising coercive control: An introduction. In M. McMahon & P. McGorrery (Eds.), *Criminalising Family Violence: Family Violence and the Criminal Law* (pp. 3–32). Singapore: Springer Nature Singapore Pte Ltd. doi:https://doi.org/10.1007/978-981-15-0653-6

Mitra-Kahn, T., Newbigin, C., & Hardefeldt, S. (2016). *Invisible Women, Invisible Violence: Understanding and Improving Data on the Experiences of Domestic and Family Violence and Sexual Assault for Diverse Groups of Women: State of Knowledge Paper*. Retrieved from Sydney: http://media.aomx.com/anrows.org.au/DiversityData_UPDATED191216.pdf

Neave, M. (2020). Foreword. In M. McMahon, & P. McGorrery (Eds.), *Criminalising Coercive Control: Family Violence and Criminal Law* (pp. v–vii). Singapore: Springer Nature Singapore Pte Ltd.

NSW Domestic Violence Death Review Team. (2020). *Report 2017–2019*. Retrieved from Lidcombe NSW: https://coroners.nsw.gov.au/documents/reports/2017-2019_DVDRT_Report.pdf

NSW Government. (2020). *Coercive Control: Discussion Paper*. Retrieved from http://www.crimeprevention.nsw.gov.au/domesticviolence/Documents/domestic-violence/discussion-paper-coercive-control.pdf

Nyman, C. (2003). The social nature of money: Meanings of money in Swedish Families. *Women's Studies International Forum*, 26(1), 79–94.

Olsberg, D., & Winters, M. (2005). *Ageing in Place: Intergenerational and Intrafamilial Housing Transfers and Shifts in Later Life*. Retrieved from https://www.ahuri.edu.au/__data/assets/pdf_file/0020/2918/AHURI_RAP_Issue_67_Ageing_in_Place.pdf

Our Watch, Australia's National Research Organisation for Women's Safety (ANROWS), & VicHealth. (2015). *Change the Story: A Shared Framework for the Primary Prevention of Violence Against Women and Their Children in Australia*. Retrieved from Melbourne: https://media-cdn.ourwatch.org.au/wp-content/uploads/sites/2/2019/05/21025429/Change-the-story-framework-prevent-violence-women-children-AA-new.pdf

Pahl, J. (1989). *Money and Marriage*. London: Macmillan.

Pahl, J. (2008). Family finances, individualisation, spending patterns and access to credit. *The Journal of Socio-Economics*, 37(2), 577–591. doi:http://dx.doi.org/10.1016/j.socec.2006.12.041

Parreñas, R. S. (2005). *Children of Global Migration: Transnational Families and Gendered Woes*. Stanford, CA: Stanford University Press.

Peled, E., & Krigel, K. (2016). The path to economic independence among survivors of intimate partner violence: A critical review of the literature and courses for action. *Aggression and Violent Behavior*, 31(November-December), 127–135. doi:https://doi.org/10.1016/j.avb.2016.08.005

Pollett, S. L. (2011). Economic abuse: The unseen side of domestic violence. *NYSBA Journal*, February, 40–44. Retrieved from https://www.nycourts.gov/ip/parent-ed/pdf/economicabusenysbjournal2011_1_1.pdf

Postmus, J. L., Hoge, G. L., Breckenridge, J., Sharp-Jeffs, N., & Chung, D. (2018). Economic abuse as an invisible form of domestic violence: A multicountry review. *Trauma, Violence, & Abuse*, 1–23. doi:10.1177/1524838018764160

Postmus, J. L., Huang, C. C., & Mathisen-Stylianou, A. (2012a). The impact of physical and economic abuse on maternal mental health and parenting. *Children and Youth Services Review*, 34(9), 1922–1928. doi:https://doi.org/10.1016/j.childyouth.2012.06.005

Postmus, J. L., Plummer, S. B., McMahon, S., Murshid, N. S., & Kim, M. S. (2012b). Understanding economic abuse in the lives of survivors. *Journal of Interpersonal Violence*, 27(3), 411–430. doi: 10.1177/0886260511421669

Postmus, J. L., Plummer, S.B., & Stylianou, A. M. (2016). Measuring economic abuse in the lives of survivors: Revising the scale of economic abuse. *Violence Against Women*, 22(6), 692–703. doi:10.1177/1077801215610012

Powell, A., & Henry, N. (2017). *Sexual Violence in a Digital Age*. London: Palgrave Macmillan.

Quilter, J. (2020). Evaluating criminalisation as a strategy in relation to non-physical family violence. In M. McMahon, & P. McGorrery (Eds.), *Criminalising Coercive Control: Family Violence and the Criminal Law* (pp. 111–131). Singapore: Springer Nature Singapore Pvt Ltd.

Rahman, M. M. (2008). *Gender Dimensions of Remittances: A Study of Indonesian Domestic Workers in East and Southeast Asia*. Retrieved from Bangkok: https://www.academia.edu/9836241/Gender_Dimensions_of_Remittances_A_Study_of_Indonesian_Domestic_Workers_in_East_and_Southeast_Asia accessed 4 May 2015

Ratha, D., Kim, E. J., Plaza, S., & Seshan, G. (2021). *Migration and Development Brief 34: Resilience: COVID-19 Crisis through a Migration Lens*. Retrieved from Washington, DC: https://www.knomad.org/sites/default/files/2021-05/Migration%20and%20Development%20Brief%2034_1.pdf

Sanders, C. K. (2015). Economic abuse in the lives of women abused by an intimate partner: A qualitative study. *Violence Against Women*, 21(1), 3–29. doi:10.1177/1077801214564167

Segrave, M. (2017). *Temporary Migration and Family Violence: An Analysis of Victimisation, Vulnerability and Support*. Retrieved from https://apo.org.au/sites/default/files/resource-files/2017-10/apo-nid114311.pdf

Segrave, M., & Vitis, L. (Eds.) (2017). *Gender, Technology and Violence*. Abingdon, Oxon and New York: Routledge.

Sharp, N. (2008). *'What's yours is mine': The Different Forms of Economic Abuse and its Impact on Women and Children Experiencing Domestic Violence - Executive Summary*. Retrieved from http://www.refuge.org.uk/files/Whats-yours-is-mine-Full-Report.pdf

Sharp-Jeffs, N. (2015). *Money Matters: Research into the Extent and Nature of Financial Abuse Within Intimate Relationships in the UK*. Retrieved from http://www.refuge.org.uk/files/Money-Matters.pdf

Sharp-Jeffs, N., & Learmonth, S. (2017). *Into Plain Sight: How Economic Abuse is Reflected in Successful Prosecutions of Controlling or Coercive*

Behaviour. Retrieved from https://survivingeconomicabuse.org/wp-content/uploads/2020/12/P743-SEA-In-Plain-Sight-report_V3.pdf

Singh, S. (1997). *Marriage Money: The Social Shaping of Money in Marriage and Banking*. St. Leonards, NSW: Allen & Unwin.

Singh, S. (2009). Balancing separateness and jointness of money in relationships: The design of bank accounts in Australia and India. In Aykin, N. (ed) *Internationalization, Design and Global Development. IDGD 2009. Lecture Notes in Computer Science, vol 5623*. (pp. 505–514). Berlin, Heidelberg: Springer. https://doi.org/10.1007/978-3-642-02767-3_56

Singh, S. (2016). *Money, Migration and Family: India to Australia*. New York: Palgrave Macmillan.

Singh, S. (2019). The daughter-in-law questions remittances: Changes in the gender of remittances among Indian migrants to Australia. *Global Networks, 19*(2), 197–217. doi:https://doi.org/10.1111/glob.12215

Singh, S., & Bhandari, M. (2012). Money management and control in the Indian joint family across generations. *The Sociological Review, 60*(1), 46–67.

Singh, S., & Cabraal, A. (2014). 'Boomerang remittances' and the circulation of care: A study of Indian transnational families in Australia. In L. Baldassar, & L. Merla (Eds.), *Transnational Families, Migration and the Circulation of Care: Understanding Mobility and Absence in Family Life* (pp. 220–234). New York: Routledge.

Singh, S., & Gatina, L. (2015). Money flows two-ways between transnational families in Australia and India. *South Asian Diaspora, 7*(1), 33–47. Retrieved from http://dx.doi.org/10.1080/19438192.2014.980564

Smallwood, E. (2015). *Stepping Stones: Legal Barriers to Economic Equality after Family Violence*. Retrieved from https://www.thelookout.org.au/sites/default/files/Legal-Barriers-To-Economic-Equality-After-Family-Violence-Sept-2015.pdf

Stark, E. (2009). Rethinking coercive control. *Violence Against Women, 15*(12), 1509–1525. doi:10.1177/1077801209347452

Stark, E. (2012). Looking beyond domestic violence: Policing coercive control. *Journal of Police Crisis Negotiations, 12*(2), 199–217. doi:10.1080/15332586.2012.725016

Stark, E. (2020). The 'coercive control framework': Making law work for women. In M. McMahon, & P. McGorrery (Eds.), *Criminalising Coercive Control: Family Violence and the Criminal Law* (pp. 33–49). Singapore: Springer Nature Singapore Pte Ltd.

Stark, E., & Hester, M. (2019). Coercive control: Update and review. *Violence Against Women, 25*(1), 81–104. doi:10.1177/1077801218816191

State of Victoria. (2016). *Getting it Done: Victorian Budget 16/17 - Service Delivery*. Retrieved from Melbourne: http://budgetfiles201617.budget.vic.gov.au/2016-17+State+Budget+-+BP3+Service+Delivery.pdf

State of Victoria Royal Commission into Family Violence. (2014–2016). *Report and Recommendations*. Retrieved from http://rcfv.archive.royalcommission.vic.gov.au/MediaLibraries/RCFamilyViolence/Reports/Final/RCFV-Vol-V.pdf

State of Victoria Royal Commission into Family Violence. (2016). *Summary and Recommendations*. Retrieved from http://rcfv.archive.royalcommission.vic. gov.au/MediaLibraries/RCFamilyViolence/Reports/RCFV_Full_Report_Interactive.pdf

Straus, M. A., Gelles, R. J., & Steinmetz, S. K. (1980). *Behind Closed Doors: Violence in the American Family*. New York: Anchor Books.

Stylianou, A. M., Postmus, J. L., & McMahon, S. (2013). Measuring abusive behaviors: Is economic abuse a unique form of abuse? *Journal of Interpersonal Violence*, 28(16), 3186–3204.

Surviving Economic Abuse and Standard Life Foundation. (2021). *The Cost of Covid-19: Economic Abuse Throughout the Pandemic*. Retrieved from https://survivingeconomicabuse.org/wp-content/uploads/2021/04/SEA-Cost-of-Covid-Report_2021-04.pdf

Tolmie, J. R. (2018). Coercive control: To criminalize or not to criminalize? *Criminology & Criminal Justice*, 18(1), 50–66. Retrieved from https://journals.sagepub.com/doi/pdf/10.1177/1748895817746712

Tuerkheimer, D. (2004). Recognising and remedying the harm of battering: A call to criminalize domestic violence. *Journal of Criminal Law and Criminology*, 94(4), 970–1032. Retrieved from https://scholarlycommons.law.northwestern.edu/cgi/viewcontent.cgi?article=7169&context=jclc

Vaughan, C., Davis, E., Murdolo, A., Chen, J., Murray, L., Block, K., Quiazon, R., & Warr, D. (2016). *Promoting Community-Led Responses to Violence Against Immigrant and Refugee Women in Metropolitan and Regional Australia. The ASPIRE Project: Key Findings and Future Directions*. Retrieved from Sydney: https://www.anrows.org.au/publication/promoting-community-led-responses-to-violence-against-immigrant-and-refugee-women-in-metropolitan-and-regional-australia-the-aspire-project-research-summary/

VicHealth. (2014). *Australians' Attitudes to Violence against Women: Findings from the 2013 National Community Attitudes towards Violence Against Women Survey (NCAS)*. Retrieved from Melbourne: https://www.vichealth.vic.gov.au/media-and-resources/publications/2013-national-community-attitudes-towards-violence-against-women-survey

Vogler, C. (1998). Money in the household: Some underlying issues of power. *The Sociological Review*, 46(4), 687–713.

Vogler, C., & Pahl, J. (1993). Social and economic change and the organisation of money within marriage. *Work, Employment and Society*, 7(1), 71–95.

Walklate, S., & Fitz-Gibbon, K. (2019). The criminalisation of coercive control: the power of law? *International Journal for Crime, Justice and Social Democracy*, 8(4), 94–108. Retrieved from https://www.crimejusticejournal.com/article/view/1205/831

Wangmann, J. (2020). Coercive control as the context for intimate partner violence: The challenge for the legal system. In M. McMahon, & P. McGorrery (Eds.), *Criminalising Family Violence: Family Violence and the Criminal Law* (pp. 218–242)). Singapore: Springer Nature Singapore Pte Ltd.

Webster, K. (2016). *A Preventable Burden: Measuring and Addressing the Prevalence and Health Impacts of Intimate Partner Violence in Australian Women: Key Findings and Future Directions*. Retrieved from Sydney, NSW: https://20ian81kynqg38bl3l3eh8bf-wpengine.netdna-ssl.com/wp-content/uploads/2019/01/28-10-16-BOD-Compass.pdf

Wherry, F. F. (2016). Relational accounting: A cultural approach. *American Journal of Cultural Sociology*, *4*, 131–156. doi:10.1057/ajcs.2016.1

Wherry, F. F. (2017). How relational accounting matters. In N. Bandelj, F. F. Wherry, & V. Zelizer (Eds.), *Money Talks: Explaining How Money Really Works* (pp. 57–69). Princeton: Princeton University Press.

Wiener, C. (2017). Seeing What is 'Invisible in Plain Sight': Policing coercive control. *The Howard Journal of Crime and Justice*, 1–16. doi:10.1111/hojo.12227

Wiener, C. (2020). From social construct to legal innovation: the offence of controlling or coercive behaviour in England and Wales. In M. McMahon, & P. McGorrery (Eds.), *Criminalising Coercive Control: Family Violence and the Criminal Law* (pp. 159–175)). Singapore: Springer Nature Singapore Pvt Ltd.

Wilkis, A. (2018). *The Moral Power of Money: Morality and Economy in the Life of the Poor*. Stanford, Calif: Stanford University Press.

Zelizer, V. A.(1985). *Pricing the Priceless Child: The Changing Social Value of Children*. New York: Basic Books.

Zelizer, V. A. (1994). *The Social Meaning of Money*. New York: Basic Books

Zelizer, V. A. (2005). *The Purchase of Intimacy*. Princeton, N.J: Princeton University Press.

Zelizer, V. A. (2011a). *Economic Lives: How Culture Shapes the Economy*. Princeton, N.J: Princeton University Press.

Zelizer, V. A. (2011b, January 27). The gender of money. *The Wall Street Journal*. Retrieved from http://blogs.wsj.com/ideas-market/2011/01/27/the-gender-of-money/

Zelizer, V. A. (2012). How I became a relational economic sociologist and what does that mean? *Politics & Society*, *40*(2), 145–174. doi:10.1177/0032329212441591

2 Carol

The joint account becomes a medium of abuse

Introduction

I knew Carol[1] through my personal networks, but I had not heard her story till I went to her home in 2016. Carol, 67, was a teacher when her 20-year first marriage ended. She was still grieving the end of her marriage when her first husband died in 1992. Seven months later, she bumped into a man she had known when she was a teenager. He began calling her, inviting her to visit him interstate. She thought it was so 'exotic.' After being wooed for seven months, Carol married her second husband Carl.

Old friends and family who knew Carl tried to warn her that he was a 'ratbag.' But her new friends and colleagues were charmed. He 'seduced them. This was part of his character. Charm and outgoing... He'd fooled them,' Carol said.

> See it's this romantic line. ...To think that you give up everything for the Knight in the White Shining Armour. It was ridiculous... But I had actually bought that line... I was so desperate after what had happened with [my first husband].

At one level she knew she was submerging who she really was. Knowing Carl thought journals were 'rubbish' she had burnt hers. Carol gave her sister her 'quiet, gentle, reflective, meditative type of music,' knowing Carl would not stand it. She left some of her books behind.

In the limousine to the church, Carol's youngest son said, 'Mum, if ever things don't go right, [my brother] and I will support you. Know

---

1 The names are pseudonyms. Some details have been generalised to ensure confidentiality.

DOI: 10.4324/9781003178606-2

that.' They got to the church itself and Carol's best friend said, 'It's not too late to change your mind.' Carol laughs. 'I wasn't listening to any of it.' She gets up for a tissue and says, 'It was too late.'

Carol knew she had made a mistake on the second night when she recognised there would be no dialogue and sharing in this marriage. But truly groomed – the first stage of coercive control – they moved interstate to Carl's home.

A joint account minus the morality of partnership in a marriage

Carol gave Carl all her savings to put in their joint account. These savings included money her sons had given her from their father's estate. These savings were enough for a deposit for a house she had hoped to buy.

I ask whether she had any qualms giving all her money to Carl. Carol says 'No. No. Well, I thought he was a Christian.' She had had a joint account in her first marriage. Money had never been a problem. She did not question that being married meant they had a joint account. 'That was my model of a marriage...I gave Carl everything. ... He didn't *actually* ask for it.'

Carol was not unusual for her generation in Anglo-Celtic culture in Australia in seeing a joint account as part of being married. In her generation, the joint account had become the symbol of togetherness in marriage. It was the single most important change in the way money was managed and controlled among middle-income Anglo-Celtic couples. This change happened partly because more women had gone into paid work from the 1950s onwards. The ideology of marriage changed to emphasise partnership, though the Christian idea of the man as head of the household remained (Singh, 1997).

In the first year, Carol was not in regular paid work, and did some relief teaching. That money also went into the joint account. 'I don't feel like I would have seen it,' she says. Carl also did not have a regular job. He was not trained for anything in particular and had worked in a medley of fields.

Carl used the money she had put into the joint account for a deposit on a house. They lived well and would go out for dinner frequently. He would go overseas for his church work.

Carol is surprised how tearful she is talking of things that are now more than ten years old. This specially surprises her for she is in a good place in her third marriage. She is sitting in a wing chair in a beautiful unit, not far from the centre of Melbourne.

She goes back to her life with Carl, saying that control 'was in the whole culture of the relationship.' He controlled the money. Even before they married, he came over to her house and sold her first husband's car. 'He said "*We* will sell that." So, he comes [from interstate] and *he* sold it. *I* didn't have anything to do with it.' He kept the money.

In the first year, Carol had no money in hand. She says, 'I had nothing at all.' Carl said to Carol she could have a credit card. Carol says 'I wouldn't *dare* spend, wouldn't *dare* spend it on anything without speaking to him. So I bought groceries [knowing] he would check, [that] he would go over the statements.'

Isolation, fear, entrapment and loss of self

Carol says the first six weeks of the marriage were difficult. She did not have a key to the house. He had a mobile phone, and she did not. As there was no land line, she had to ask him if she could make an interstate call. He would say, 'No.' She says, 'If he had known about brainwashing ... I would have thought he had deliberately done this to me.' She does not think he 'had a clue of how you brainwash people, how you make people feel disenfranchised and disempowered. But this is exactly what he did.'[2]

He did not want her to keep her books in the house. She had some in a back room that he did not see. He 'would not allow me to write a journal. So, I'd have to do that, without him knowing. And then I'd feel terribly guilty. Isn't that ridiculous?' Books and writing were core to her life. She says, 'I didn't know that life existed like that, that you could be treated so abysmally. So, there was real abuse ... it was psychological, verbal.'

In those first months, Carol felt, 'I've burnt my bridges now...I had really done my dash.' She had not listened to her family and friends who tried to warn her. And now she could not phone them. She was not yet teaching and felt,

> ... cut off from everything. I remember, I don't know how long I'd been there, six months or so, I was desperate to talk to another Victorian. That's how migrants feel.... Have you ever felt that you just wanted to talk with your own tribe? I just wanted to speak with someone. I wanted connection ... I'd never been treated like that before. I just needed someone.

---

2 See Hill (2019) and Stark (2007) for similarities between brainwashing and family violence.

Carl was isolating her from her family, an important precondition for coercive control. He tried to prevent her from visiting her sons. He got rid of things she loved. He sold Carol's sewing machine that she had had for years, which allowed her to do some complicated sewing. He sold it without telling her. He would have sold her books but most remained interstate.

She had a roll top desk. She says, 'I adored everything about it. It was very special to me.' He reluctantly agreed to her having it in the bedroom, but

> ... wouldn't have it in the lounge area or anywhere else.... I think a roll top desk is a beautiful thing, like a piano or something.... and then he decided we would have a garage sale and *that* would go in the garage sale. What I said, made no difference.

There was the looming threat of physical violence. She had worked out she could curl up in the big walk-in wardrobe to escape him. She says,

> There were a few occasions when I actually hid from him, curled up (in the walk-in wardrobe). There was room for me and he wouldn't know where I was and couldn't see me. I hid like that for about three hours. I think I knew that he was going to turn on me....I heard him calling me. He'd calmed down by the time I emerged. He didn't even really ask me where I'd been.

She says she began to lose her mind. 'There were a few times before, that I'd nearly gone crazy.' She didn't, for she knew her youngest son 'supported me so much. It is his love that I could feel and the love of God that stopped me.'

Carol started working the second year. She says,

> He took it all. He took it all and that paid off the house we were in. All my pay paid off the house we were in. We built this beautiful home that was supposed to be my dream home but in reality, I had very little to do with it.

She realised she had no freedom. She could not use her money as she wanted. The car she drove was his. What she minded most was not being able to give generous gifts to her family and friends. Even though she was earning, he tried to prevent her from visiting her sons.

When her sons sent her $15,000,[3] she opened a separate account, a 'sneaky account.' She felt 'a bit unfaithful ... I knew that lots of women do this, but I never thought I'd be in the position.'

Deciding to leave

She decided to leave within two and a half years of her marriage – and only after friends voiced their suspicions of criminality around her husband's overseas trips. She then directed her pay to her separate account. But she did not feel free enough to take any money out of the joint account.

Despite her dominant contributions to the house, in the financial settlement she received only 40 per cent of the house and one of the two cars. Her lawyer said she could fight, but Carol walked away. She thought it would cost another $20,000 and she may still lose.

Reflecting on what made her stay, Carol says she 'was truly sticking with it because I'd made these vows.' Her first marriage was not meant to break down, for a divorce was abhorrent to her. She told herself this marriage was going to work. Carol says, 'I thought in my naiveté that if I loved him so much then he would love me, and it would all be alright.'

He asked her to massage him when he came back from work. Though she is not a 'touchy feely' person, and she is embarrassed about it, he would lie on the floor and she would massage him for an hour or two. She laughs and says she was probably not good at the massage. But she would 'exhaust' herself and think that 'love might overcome.'

However, she knew 'from day one or day two' that it was going to be difficult. She was pouring it out in her journal that she was hiding from Carl. She says, 'I didn't know how I was going to survive. I sure prayed, heaps. And I went to counselling and I would pour out to friends and ask for help.'

Carol established friendships when she started teaching. She eventually talked of what was happening at home with a couple who understood and listened. She was able to leave knowing her family would be supportive. Her friends and colleagues also encouraged her to leave. It was a small community. The school principal and the church pastor told her to leave the marriage. She says,

> Everybody in the church was wonderful. Everybody understood. The pastor certainly wasn't the kind who would support divorce

---

3   The money is in Australian dollars.

... but he understood the whole situation. I had been to him for help before this and after. He was wonderful.

Carol is fortunate to have received support from her faith community. The State of Victoria Royal Commission into Family Violence noted in volume 5 (State of Victoria Royal Commission into Family Violence, 2014–2016) '... that women experiencing family violence can face barriers to seeking help within their faith communities as a result of particular religious beliefs and practices' (p. 131).

Carol taught in the same state for a year after her marriage ended, to make sure she had made the right decision.

When she moved back to Victoria, she returned to teaching in school, gained another degree, and a language. She moved into her own house, which she renovated and learnt gardening. She 're-established and reinvented herself'.

Her story ends joyfully for she happily married again, six years after she left Carl.

This time too, Carol gave her husband her savings of some $60,000 and they bought a house together, though he had another two properties. Her contribution was mainly in cash but overall was less than his. This time, her husband had the morality to see their marriage and money as a shared enterprise.

She stopped working five years after she married and feels grateful for the stability she has. They have two joint accounts and each of them also has a separate account. Her husband transfers a set amount to her account every month, so she has money in hand.

He is very Christian in his behaviour and attitudes and that is important to her. He is a great grandfather to her grandchildren. She says, 'I am grateful all the time. I know. I KNOW what men can be now and I am so grateful now. And I know that it makes a difference to be positive too.'

Carol asks if I can stay for dinner and see for myself that he is 'the most honourable person you could ever meet and very generous....' Her family loves him too. She laughs, 'I have learned to be more discerning, more critical.' She adds, she has also learnt from her husband 'not to judge, but to accept situations and people much more.'

References

Hill, J. (2019). *See What You Made Me Do: Power, Control and Domestic Violence*. Collingwood, Australia: Schwartz Publishing Pty, Limited.

Singh, S. (1997). *Marriage Money: The Social Shaping of Money in Marriage and Banking.* St. Leonards, NSW: Allen & Unwin.

Stark, E. (2007). *Coercive Control: The Entrapment of Women in Personal Life.* New York: Oxford University Press.

State of Victoria Royal Commission into Family Violence. (2014–2016). *Report and Recommendations: Volume V.* Retrieved from http://rcfv.archive.royalcommission.vic.gov.au/MediaLibraries/RCFamilyViolence/Reports/Final/RCFV-Vol-V.pdf

3 Ekta

The 'good son' sends her money to his parents

Introduction

I met Ekta[1], 27, in 2010, through a colleague who had known her in India. We met at the vocational institute where she was teaching. I was interviewing her to learn of her migration experience as a student for an earlier study 'Money, Migration and Family.' Her story is of a woman who has struggled against economic and emotional abuse in marriage and re-established herself. But it is only while telling her story she saw her husband's use of money without morality and care as a central issue in her marriage. Even then, she did not speak of economic abuse or family violence.

Ekta came to Australia in 2005 on a student visa. That was not her original intention for she had done her Master of Accounting and another Master of Finance, and had been working for three years in the finance sector. Her ambition was to do a PhD from a good university in Australia. She applied for permanent residence (PR) from India.

When her papers for PR were ready, some family friends said, 'Oh, don't send your daughter alone there.' This is a usual refrain in many of the stories of women migrants who are the principal applicants. The fear is that a woman alone in a foreign land will get into trouble. The woman also becomes a passport for a man who himself is unable to qualify for migration.

Family friends found a boy who was already in Australia. He was from the same *Jat* caste and owned land. Ekta agreed, but wanted to go only when she had PR. She had her degrees assessed for eligibility. But her fiancé's parents insisted she should go first on a student's visa.

---

1 The names are pseudonyms. Some of the details have been generalised to ensure confidentiality.

DOI: 10.4324/9781003178606-3

Ekta's mother bowed to the pressure. Ekta's father had died when she was 12 and Ekta's nuclear family was small with just her mother and younger sister. Ekta got engaged in June 2005, left for Australia in November and they were married in December 2005. In 2006, she enrolled for a semester in university.

The early days of marriage were good. But in March 2006, her husband received a letter from Immigration, deporting him for he had overstayed his visa. On the same day Ekta found she was pregnant. She did not want to believe he had married her for the visa.

He and his family wanted her to abort the child, but she resisted. She went to stay with her cousin in Sydney. Her daughter was born in November 2006, and she got her PR in January 2007.

She went to India with her daughter for two or three months, but her husband did not come to stay with her. Ekta's mother told her not to sponsor her husband. But Ekta thought he was alright. He had just been influenced by his parents. She returned to Australia and sent the sponsorship papers.

Economic abuse and conflicting moralities of money

Her husband came back to Australia in December 2007. By that time, Ekta was working at a bank and on the weekends was working at Coles. She was excited about her husband's return, but it was not as she had imagined. There were fights every day. He ignored her and their daughter.

Her husband controlled the money, which was in a joint account. He would continually ask, 'Why did you spend a dollar there?' In 2008, he began working. The rent and household expenses came out of her salary. He sent all his salary home and some of hers without consultation.

There were conflicting moralities around remittances. Ekta's husband prioritised the welfare of his parents over that of his wife and daughter. Ekta says his parents lived like maharajas, while in Australia, Ekta was working very hard and struggling. His parents also wanted dowry though Ekta had made it clear when they got married, there was going to be no dowry.

She kept thinking his family was influencing him. She says, for her, 'Money was not an issue in my married life.... If he had looked after my daughter and I, I would have been happy ... but when nothing was working out, then money also became an issue.' It was not just the control of money, but control without care and morality that made the control coercive.

Ekta was teary most of the time recounting the kindness of her work mates and bosses at the bank and Coles during this time. The manager at Coles was more like a friend and knew of her troubles. She is also close to his family. He advised her to leave her husband saying, 'If he does not care for you, leave him.'

Her boss at the bank and the team – they told her they would work around her schedules. She did not have a car at the time. It was difficult for her to leave at 5pm, and pick up her daughter at the other end of the city by 6 pm. Some of her teammates would go shopping during their lunch break, and buy her daughter gifts.

Her Greek neighbour was like a mother to her. She worried about Ekta. She could hear the fights and told Ekta 'If you are in trouble, call me, and I'll call the police.'

Her 19-year-old sister came to study and stay with them on a student visa in April 2008. Ekta's husband insisted, against the norms of family relationship, that Ekta's mother pay one fourth the rent and household expenses. Ekta said that 'pinched me.' She told her husband, 'You are spending so much on your family. Why can't I spend? We can at least help support our family.' That began another fight.

By this time, Ekta says, 'There was no physical relationship ... I felt I was just a maid, cooking for him, doing everything for him and giving all my money to him.' She says,

> My sister saw everything. She said, "No. This is not life." She informed Mummy. I never said anything. I said, "Okay. Maybe he will change." I was just waiting and watching, but she said, "No. You have to step up. He can't change totally." I was, "No, no, no. He'll be okay. He'll be okay."

Ekta was suicidal but her family and friends told her to hold on, that everything would be alright. Then Ekta's sister overheard Ekta's husband and parents talking on the phone, saying the strategy was for him to get PR – he was still on a provisional spouse visa – and then he could ditch his wife. He would then marry again and get a large dowry. They told him, "Don't worry. Get your residency and after that we will see what we have to do."

The marriage ends

In 2008, less than three years into her marriage, Ekta, her daughter and sister walked out of the house with only a few clothes for the baby. He did not try and stop her, or hold on to the baby. He told her if she walks out of the house, she would not be allowed to come back. He had already emptied their joint bank account.

They went to the home of Ekta's friend from her kindergarten days. They used to be next door neighbours when she was five years old and he was three. Just 12 days before, Ekta was surfing Orkutt and came across him and found he was in Melbourne. He came over to meet her. When he learnt of her desperation, he gave her his number and told her to come whenever she needed.

Ekta called him and they all went to his one bedroom flat. He left the fully furnished flat to them and moved out to a friend's place. As she had no money, he gave her his card and told her to get whatever she needed. In a month or so, her mother sent her money, and she was able to return all of it. She says for her, he was like God himself to have been there for their support.

Even then, Ekta hoped her husband might come back. He knew where she was working but he did not try to contact her. Then Ekta's childhood friend's father happened to be posted as an election officer in her husband's village. He learnt from her husband's brother that the family was looking for a well-off girl to be a bride for their son. They were open about their desire to get a dowry.

When Ekta heard, she withdrew her sponsorship of her husband in June 2009. By this time, she was an Australian citizen. It was then, her husband began calling her. But Ekta filed for divorce. However, before the divorce came through, her husband was able to get a visitor's visa to the US where he had relatives. He told them he would not overstay as he had a wife and daughter in Melbourne, and his wife was a citizen.

Ekta, her sister and daughter left the friend's flat after staying there a year. She left her job at the bank just before her divorce because she was not able to cope with the stress of the divorce and the job. She moved to teaching though the salary was lower, but the hours were better.

Her mother has visited three times and they rent their own flat. When I happened on her again in 2019, she had her own car and was teaching in vocational education in a university in Melbourne. If I see her again, I will ask whether she did her PhD.

4 Rina

Dowry is economic, emotional and physical abuse

Introduction: The parents give dowry

I spoke with Rina,[1] 27, in 2017 in my office. That was a more private space for her than her workplace, or the room she rents from a family. I got in touch with her through a person who knew those who had supported her when she left her marriage.

Rina has a BA Honours. She worked in hospitality in a managerial position in India, before she got married to an Indian who lived in Australia in 2016. She saw herself as independent and strong willed.

Rina comes from a conservative business family who live in a middle-income suburb in a metropolitan city. It was an arranged marriage. Rina and her future husband corresponded for four months, and met each other a week before the wedding.

Two days before the wedding in India, the groom's parents demanded gold, cash, and a car as dowry. Relatives and friends advised Rina's family not to accede to their demands fearing that once they had asked, they would continue asking. Rina herself did not believe in dowry, but she liked the groom and thought him charming and respectful. He would open the door for her.

Her parents were hesitant. They asked, 'Is he nice to you?' The wedding preparations went ahead. Rina's parents refused the car and cash but gave gold gifts to the extended family, including the husband's maternal grandmother, the father-in-law's brother, and his wife. Her parents thought dowry would not be a continuing issue as Rina would be going to Australia, and not be living with her husband's parents in India.

---

1 The names are pseudonyms. Some of the details have been generalised to ensure confidentiality.

DOI: 10.4324/9781003178606-4

However, four days after the wedding, her husband's family assaulted her verbally and emotionally that the dowry was inadequate. The father-in-law and the mother-in-law continued to accuse her family of not conducting a proper marriage, of not giving the customary gifts for festivals.

There were arguments when Rina was with her husband at his parents' place. She says,

> He started throwing things. I saw his violent nature, which I never knew existed. He started pulling his hair, hitting his head with his slippers, and hitting his head against the wall. He started calling me names, cursing me, abusing me.

Later, when they went to her parents' house for dinner and to stay the night, her husband got angry at something. 'It was 1.30 in the night. He threatened to commit suicide. My house is on 10th floor. He went to the balcony and created a scene.' The security guards saw him shouting and screaming as Rina begged him to go inside.

Rina's brother asked what had happened. She told him they were sorting out some issues. 'He asked, "Are you sure?" Rina said, "Yes".' Her parents did not know of it as their room was shut because the air conditioner was on that summer night.

Rina stayed with her parents for a month and a half before leaving for Australia. They saw her looking unhappy and sensed something was wrong. They asked her many times whether everything was fine, whether she wanted to go to Australia. Rina told them it was all fine. She said, 'It's just that I am upset leaving you behind.' They believed her.

Rina came on a tourist visa, after applying for a Spouse Visa.

Coercive control through isolation, economic, emotional, and physical abuse

In Australia, Rina's husband pushed her to find work, saying he had borrowed $10,000[2] to bring her to Australia. He was not happy at work and accused her of staying idly at home. At least she could try and find him another job. He got a new job, but things remained tense at home.

He accused Rina of not knowing how to cook. She says,

> I was new to the kitchen. I forgot to put the lid on the cooker when I made the lentils. He would come to the kitchen and say, 'Is the

---

2 The money is in Australian dollars.

food ready? Leave it, let's go out to eat.' After eating when we came home, he would see the food lying outside. He used to say, 'Didn't you keep the food inside? You don't even know that much? Nobody taught you anything. What did your mother teach you before sending you here?' I used to say 'Sorry.' Just then he would start breaking glass etc. saying, 'I am sick of you.'

His parents knew their son was violent and were afraid of him. Rina suggested she and her husband see a marriage counsellor, but her husband refused.

The physical abuse started after three months. He pulled her elbow, pulled her hair, pushed her to the kitchen wall. It happened every week. He was suspicious of everybody she spoke with. Rina says,

> He started accusing me of having a relationship with every person that I spoke to. Even when I went for a walk outside, he asked, 'Whom were you talking to?' I would say, 'Just somebody who was asking the way.' He would say 'Ok. So, you must have given your number too.'

The physical and emotional abuse was accompanied by economic abuse and isolation. When they fought, he would 'snatch my phone saying that he pays the bill, so I have no right to talk to anybody. He used to go out with my phone, and I used to feel very helpless that in an alien country, where do I go and whom do I speak to.'

Rina did not have money or a bank account. In the first six months, Rina's husband gave her only $100. She was not employed. She did not have money in hand to go anywhere on public transport. She did not have a credit card. Most of her jewellery was kept in a bank locker under her father-in-law's name in India. She never got it back.

She told her parents about the physical abuse. Her mother at first told her to adjust, that it would become better. Rina told her husband's sister, but she said it was okay to be abusive. Her father-in-law called her names. Her mother-in-law complained that her family had not given her enough.

She did not know anybody in Melbourne in the first few months. They went to the Sikh temple every week. She said 'Everybody knew him...If I had told somebody, they would have said, "Are you mad? He is such a nice boy".'

Her mother's first cousin lived on the other side of the city. Rina had not met him and did not tell him anything. She says she was traumatised. She did not want to go back to India. She felt that after marriage, her parents' home was not hers. Her husband's home is not hers. So, does she have a home at all?

Five months after Rina came to Australia, her father-in-law told her to tell her father to send her a ticket to go back to India. He said '"They don't want a daughter-in-law like me"... He used to ask his son to send me back, saying, "There is no place for her in Australia".'

Rina's father booked a ticket in half an hour.

She went back for two months to India. None of her friends and family understood why she had tolerated so much. She was so independent.

Despite her parents' objections, Rina returned because her husband asked her to come back. She wanted to give her relationship another chance.

Rina feared she would be found dead

The situation worsened. Her husband continued to be abusive. 'He deleted all my contacts from the phone – parents, brother, friends so that I'm not in touch with anybody. He deleted my WhatsApp.'

A month after Rina returned, her temporary spouse visa arrived. Rina's husband pressured her to begin work. Her husband had a separate account. He consulted his family who advised him to open a joint account for her. Rina suggested they ask the bank consultant.

At the bank, the consultant said, the 'joint account is better for a loan. My husband said, "Let's open her joint account." The bank consultant said, "No, it is your account that gets joint by adding her name to it".' Her husband baulked. He kept his separate account and opened a separate account for her. He deposited $100 in it, but that day he used her debit card to spend $45 on groceries.

She went for job interviews. Though she had managerial experience in India, she was not successful. Rina said, 'I had no confidence at all. I was very weak and demoralised. I lost who I was.'

Her husband accused her of being inauspicious saying that when she stepped into his parents' house after marriage, the lights went out. He told her many times she was unlucky and a disgrace to his family. He said he 'felt embarrassed walking with me.'

Her husband became more abusive, accusing her of eating all day at home without work. They went for dinner, after which he parked in a secluded car park. He continued to abuse her and her family. He said she would feel the abuse only if,

> I hit you with a stick. (He will) force me to have sex with him. Your father must have raped your mother so you think it happens everywhere. He called my Mom names and that

was enough for me. He called my Mom a whore and my Dad a pimp, my brother an adopted child .... I couldn't take anymore. I knew it was over. I felt whatever I may do for him, he will never be satisfied. He threatened to hit me when we reached home. I couldn't breathe .... I was getting worried about my safety. I felt if I stayed there another night, I would be found dead the next day.

Rina did not know how she had come to this. She had always wanted to marry and be loved like her parents who loved each other. Her Dad respected her mother. She told herself she had been so strong willed. She did not deserve anything like this.

When they reached home, he went inside angrily. She stood outside and called her mother. Her husband came out to ask her who she was calling. She told him she was calling her mother. He said, 'Tell her I will beat you tonight.'

Her mother consulted her cousin in Melbourne who advised Rina to call the police. She was worried about the effect on her relationship. Her uncle asked, 'Do you still want to continue the relationship?'

Two policemen came in about half an hour. By that time, her husband had gone out. When he came back, he found the police there. They had filed an intervention order. He collected his clothes. He also took her jewellery that was in the house. She eventually got back a ring and bangles. All the rest was taken.

Her marriage was over within a year.

Rina went to live for a while with her uncle's family. He put her in touch with a multicultural service provider dealing with family violence. She also saw a psychiatrist. She applied for permanent residence through the provider and got it.

Her first reaction was to return to India, leaving behind her experience of abuse in Australia. Her mother's cousin in Australia spoke to a Justice of Peace he knew, who warned them that Rina's husband would never change. He advised Rina to stay in Australia and make a life for herself.

Rina says, 'I'm completely independent now. I'm not dependent on anyone now. Initially my parents transferred $500 to my account. But after a month and a half, I got my job.' She interviewed for five jobs and got each one of them.

The first two weeks were difficult. Her supervisor sensed something was not right and asked if everything was alright in her personal life. She confided her problems and within two months began to concentrate on her job.

She moved out of her uncle's house and rented a room with an Indian family in the same suburb. She feels independent again, in control of her money. She is saving to buy a house. She has work colleagues but still does not have friends. Weekends are spent doing the laundry, shopping for groceries. Rina says,

> I am seeing the city now. I used to hate this place, a place that tortured me. I used to cry every day. It wasn't a beautiful place for me. Now I have regained my confidence. I'm not dependent on someone who calls me names, who used to think that I can't do anything. I have started loving this place. I don't want to go to India now. This is my place. This is my home now.

5 Geeta
He gave me coins, not notes

Introduction

I met Geeta[1] through an organisation supporting Indians suffering family violence. We spoke in her unit in an Indian part of the city. The smell of curry was in the stairwell. Her daughter was watching TV in the living room. I could hear food cooking in the pressure cooker.

Geeta, in her late 30s, has an MBA and worked as a Human Resources professional in South India before she married her husband. She has two children and was married for ten years. This was her second marriage, after her first marriage disintegrated within the first year.

The second marriage was initially arranged through a Marriage Bureau. Her father asked to see Geeta's husband's salary statement. When he did not show it, her father withdrew his approval. But Geeta's husband convinced her sister-in-law that he really cared for her.

Geeta married against her father's wishes. They eloped the next day. She wanted this second chance to have a husband and family.

Her husband worked in information technology in Australia. When she moved with her husband to Australia, he wanted her to stay home. Within six months, she was pregnant.

The initial period of grooming also coincided with her increasing isolation. She had no family or friends in Australia. Her husband took away her Indian mobile phone so she could not talk to her parents in India. He did not give her the key to the letter box and read her family's letters to her. He also kept her passport and her Medicare card.

---

1 The names are pseudonyms. Some of the details have been generalised to ensure confidentiality.

DOI: 10.4324/9781003178606-5

Coercive control leads to a total deprivation of freedom

Geeta had to ask her husband for money. She knew he was stingy. She says, 'He was not giving me any notes, just coins.' She had never gone alone in a train because it cost $8.[2] She says, 'It was his wish whatever he wants to buy, he'll buy for us. It's like that. And whatever he likes me to wear, I have to wear.' He had the ATM card for her bank account and knew the password. But she says, 'I trusted him ... I was held up with household duties. He got the groceries and paid the bills.'

After the first child she went into postnatal depression. She says, 'I didn't know what was happening with me. I thought "It's Australia, new place, I have to listen to him."' She adds, 'I never questioned him.'

She tried to please him by giving him a good breakfast, and then asked for $20–30. From this, she saved money and walked to Target and bought a $40 mobile. He smashed her phone. Though Geeta had no mobile phone, her husband had four iPhones. He locked them in his bag with his laptop. There was little communication. He was very silent.

The physical violence started within the first two years. He first slapped her in the balcony in her parents' house on a visit to India. Even in his parents' house, he would hit her, and his sisters would try and stop him. Geeta would keep quiet. She thought, he takes care of everything. She told herself, 'He is my husband. I trust him....' She wavered when he said, 'You came with only one dress.'

For Geeta, the first breaking point was when her husband saw her wearing one of the long nighties her sister had sent from India. He stomped on all the nighties. It started a big fight, with her husband slapping her and saying she is useless. He went to the bedroom with a knife and slashed all the nightdresses, and then tried to pull off the one she was wearing.

He dragged her wearing the remaining nightie and threatened her with the knife. Her children, three and eight years old, were watching. He scared her with a rod. Usually, he would smile afterwards, but this time she was 'not able to take it.'

She went to her friend's unit in the next block, and they called community services. They said to call the police. The police came at 5am. The children were with the father. The police said they would arrest him, but she only wanted them to give him a warning. She went back and stayed with her husband and children.

---

2   The money is in Australian dollars.

The next physical assault was triggered when her husband refused to give Geeta $40 to pay library fines. She knew she had a bank account, but had never accessed it. She went to the bank and found there was $200 in the account. She withdrew $100.

Her husband came to know for he had third party access to her account. He also had her card and knew her password. He began beating her. She called the police again who gave him a warning.

Geeta also called two of her husband's friends telling them he will not give her anything above $50, that he is holding her letters and bank statements from India. She told them she has to beg him for money. Both his friends tried to convince him to give Geeta money, but her husband was adamant. He told Geeta before his friends, 'You are just a caretaker, and I won't give one cent of money to you.'

Thinking she could take the remaining $100 from her account to get a new Medicare card, she went to the bank and found he had withdrawn that. This is when she learnt her husband had third party access to her account. And he had her card. Geeta felt now she will have to again beg for money. But the teller told her there was a fixed deposit account in her name with $25,000.

Geeta took out the money and deposited it in a new account with no third-party access. Her husband slapped her and told her to go back to the bank. She refused. He beat her again, slamming her. He said, 'I can't trust you.' He accused her of stealing his money.

He took her to the shopping centre where the bank was located. He bought her a dress and promised to buy her a mobile. He asked her to move the money to his account. She was scared of what he would do. She was also scared of not having any money. She walked away. Geeta told him, she needed the money to study so she could get a job. He left her alone at the shopping centre saying, 'I'm leaving you. I don't trust you'.

She travelled alone by train for the first time and came home. He told her he had called the police. Early in the morning, she heard her son screaming for his father was beating him. He then slapped her face on both sides and pressed his knee on her body. He said, 'You took my money.' She called the police. This time, after advice from Community Services, she asked for an Apprehended Violence Order (AVO). Now, she says that was a mistake, for 'an AVO complicates so many things. He was arrested but came home after two hours.'

He began to live separately in another bedroom with his door locked. She had to attend a court hearing for the AVO, but the hearing was continually adjourned. There was no communication with her husband. Geeta says, 'It was like walking on eggshells.'

The AVO did not stop the violence. She found it was 'just a piece of paper.' Her husband was becoming more aggressive. He pushed her and her daughter against the bathroom door. Geeta hit her head against the toilet bowl and hurt her back. 'That's the end,' she thought. She says she thought this is not acceptable. Her body was hurting. She couldn't get up for three to four minutes.

Her husband left the bathroom and did his prayers. He then left for the office.

Geeta talked to her friends at her daughter's playgroup. Geeta cried. They told her she had to complain to the police. When Geeta said she was worried it would spoil her family life, they said she couldn't keep quiet when her husband had hurt her so. The person in charge of the playgroup went with Geeta to make a complaint at the police station.

The police came two days later and asked her husband what happened. He said he had not pushed Geeta. The police left.

There was an uneasy silence for two or three months. He would take the children and sleep with them in a closed bedroom. One night, Geeta told her husband she needed to give milk to her daughter. He opened the door and slapped her. 'You don't have patience,' he said. He told her she would 'become a beggar or a prostitute,' if he did not give her money.

Geeta was not able to hear. She went again to the playgroup and then to Relationships Australia, where she had a counselling appointment. She then went to the medical centre to have her ear checked. Like the playgroup, they advised her to go to the police.

The next day the police came. They arrested him, charged him for assault and locked him up for a week for breaching the AVO. When he was released, he came to take his things and left the house. At that point in front of the police, she took back her passport and those of her children. He would not give her the garage keys.

Her husband came back the next day. A few days later they fought, and her husband beat her again. Geeta says,

> He took the scissors, kitchen scissors. I didn't know what he was doing. The children were inside. He took the scissors. I was sitting there on the sofa, he took out the scissors and grabbed something from behind the table and in our language he said, 'I wish I could cut off your tongue. Your tongue should not be there.' Then he cut the TV wire ... It was terrible. I didn't know what to do. This is hell ... Then I went to the bedroom and ... called the police.

The police took the scissors and said, Geeta should take out an exclusion order so that her husband would have to leave the house, and Geeta and the children could continue to stay.

After recounting the physical violence, Geeta asks, 'Do you think I did wrong by taking the money? Did I do wrong to call the police?' Later she says, 'I should have complained earlier. My life would have been better.' She adds that people in India think it is her fault. Her husband has accused her of being mad.

For the next six months he did not contact the children. He accused her of being mad and applied for custody. The divorce went through in 2016. The property settlement is being fought through the courts. Whatever happens, the unit will be sold. She hopes he will soon pay child support.

Geeta says, it is only when she went to the court, she found out she had suffered family violence, that he wanted to keep her dependent.

Geeta has not discussed her problems with her family, even when he was hiding her letters. She says, 'I trusted him. It was a family matter.' She reached out to her friends and neighbours. She told his friends about the violence. She also spoke with people at the Sai Baba temple. They said they could only talk to him when he came. She went to a Support Centre. Through them, she has had someone who accompanies her to the court and to the conciliation conference.

She worries about the costs of a financial settlement through the court. She looks forward to greater independence, but this is not the result she wanted. She feels she should have complained earlier. At the same time, she blames herself for complaining at all. She is grateful for the end of violence but sad at the end of her marriage. Now her life is hurtling past divorce, through property settlement, working with lawyers. Blaming herself, she asks, 'Did I do wrong?'

6 Karen

'I've been a single mother for most of my married life'

Introduction

I hear Karen's[1] story in my office on one of the days she is in the city. She is a friend of another participant in the study.

Karen, 62, married at 24. She was a teacher. Her husband was an electrician. Karen and her husband had joint accounts. His money went for the household expenses. Her earnings were their savings for a house.

This joint management and control of money changed when Karen stopped teaching just before her daughter's birth. She chose the traditional role of mother and home maker. But within ten months her husband's work became erratic, just when his role as provider became more urgent.

Most often he did not have work. He was in and out of work, not getting on with his bosses, taking short cuts. Karen says,

> He always used to think that people were picking on him.... He might be in a job for one year and he would be out of work for nine months. Then he might have another job for two years and he would be out of work for 18 months.

When his work was 'coming and going' and he was out of employment, they bought a caravan to show films in schools in Northern NSW and Tasmania. After they came back from Tasmania, a son was born. They were on Centrelink benefits and were living in the caravan at the back of a friend's house.

---

1 The names are pseudonyms. Some of the details have been generalised to ensure confidentiality.

DOI: 10.4324/9781003178606-6

They used the friend's washing machine. The caravan had six berths. She remembers putting the son's basket on the berth and jiggling that up and down while cutting vegetables. 'I would stand in the kitchen ... I used to console myself and say this is my new mansion.... That was really hard.'

Later, they stayed in another friend's house for six months, rent free. Karen was on the receiving end of hand-me-downs and generosity from family and friends. She could see her wardrobe and know exactly where every dress had come from.

The morality of money changes across life stage

Money in Karen's marriage went according to Anglo-Celtic expectations in the first two years. They set up joint accounts and agreed on expenses and savings, reflecting the expectations of partnership in marriage. But when they had children, Karen stopped paid work expecting her husband would provide.

When her husband was not able to adequately provide, he asked Karen whether she would go out into paid work, and he could be at home. She says, 'I had grown up in the culture where women were able to go to work, but it was preferable to stay home and look after the kids.' She did apply to teach part time, but the education department did not permit it.

She had also seen that even when her husband was unemployed, he did not look after the home and children. Karen and her friends thought his offer to stay at home was a bit 'of a cop out.' She says, 'his inability to consistently provide was distressing.' She remembers telling him, 'It's really preferable that you go out to work.'

The children were under five. Her husband tried to run his own business. He would get and lose a contract, upgrade his skills. He would take short cuts or do the work not so well. One day a call came, saying, your husband has done the wrong thing, with such and such company. Karen says, it 'freaked me out.'

When he started a business, he spent the money on 'men's toys' buying CB (Citizens Band) radios, car batteries, mobile phones, and car headlights.

Karen and her husband still had joint accounts. Once he started a business, he gave her $200[2] a week, only because his secretary said he should. He got pretty 'narky' about that. From that, $50 went on the

---

2   The money is in Australian dollars.

house, $80–$100 on food. Then there were the clothes, utility bills. When the secretary left, the $200 a week stopped, with only the '"leftovers" for me. Some weeks I didn't get anything.' This went on for 18 months.

During the years of 'economic fragility,' Karen began a vegie patch. She also started piano tuitions at home at $5 for half an hour. That meant $20 a week for four students. Together with the child allowance of about $20 a month, it meant she had some money in hand.

She took over the management of the money so that her husband could not spend what he had earned on 'men's toys.' But her money soon finished. The utilities and bills had to come from him.

Economic abuse and a life of privation

Karen's husband's failure to provide plummeted her to a life of privation. When she gave private tuition, he was an obstruction rather than a support. She says, 'I've been a ... single mother for most of my married life.'

Karen says, 'It was like walking on eggshells,' never knowing how to manage. He is going to work, not going to work. It was very hard to plan.' At the same time, her daughter was not well and needed serious attention for her eyes till she was 10 years old.

He also tried to sabotage her music practice at church and teaching by coming home late. Karen told one of the ministers, 'I can't come to music practice, because then my husband would deliberately stay out.' She says, 'It was that kind of manipulation. Somebody must have spoken to him, and after that it stopped.'

Sometimes the loose change vanished. She would ask where the $5 went for they had to catch a train to the Eye and Ear Hospital for her daughter's eye treatment. Other times she knew there was $1 lying there and it wasn't.

Later, she learnt that her daughter used to take $2 from her purse, for she wanted to be like everybody else and have pies on Mondays.

It was living on a 'knife edge.' She negotiated with the secondary college, and it reduced the children's fees to a third and paid for the uniforms. She had to pay for her daughter's teeth to be fixed with braces.

She prided herself on being able to dish out a meal with an egg, rice and some leftover vegetables. 'I used to work out my shopping to the exact dollar. I was proud of myself as to what I could accomplish ... Ice cream was only for birthday parties, fish and chips for Sunday.'

For Karen it was one dollar a serve per person for meat, and the 250 grams of butter was divided into seven portions to last the week.

A lot of minced meat, sausages and if it was silverside, it was sliced thin. She adds, 'I used to go down shopping, and we all would go to the toilet,' so we did not have to press the toilet and increase the home water bill.

What continues to hurt is that she had to tell her daughter there would be no new clothes when she went to university, and not being able to afford to have her son's teeth fixed. She cries remembering that time. She says, 'The whole of my life was really awful for there was no real support. I had to be strong for me.'

As with most women, she adds, 'I put my kids first.... I put myself last.' She prioritised the children's education and health over food, clothing, furniture, and her needs. She was shocked seeing a photograph of herself during her marriage. She was 46 kgs rather than the 60 kgs she is now.

'People were generous to me, giving me clothes, things for the kids. I am a generous person too. I gave my time in music, theatre. I took the playgroup in the church for two or three years.' Karen says, often she felt she didn't have anything to share. But then she thought I have oranges on the orange tree, share the house, the car. If I have a big pile of leaves, share those.

The economic abuse was accompanied by emotional and physical abuse. Her husband began to accuse her of having affairs. Later, she learnt he was either attempting or having affairs with some of her female friends. Karen says her husband hit her once when his mother was visiting. His mother spoke sternly to him, and Karen's husband never hit her again. She wonders whether his father was also violent. She tried to probe, but her mother-in-law was silent. Only in 1998 when her mother-in-law died, she heard theirs was a dysfunctional, aggressive household.

Empowering herself through a slow reskilling and further education

The economic, emotional, and physical abuse happened within the context of an unsatisfactory marriage. Within a month of her marriage, Karen told her pastor she had made a mistake, but he said now she had made her bed, she had to lie on it. Her family and friends said the same things; adapt, adjust, you will grow to love him. 'Mum used to say, "Cheer up. Keep looking up. Rely on God's love."'

Karen grew up on a large country farm. She had a good relationship with her father and stepmother, but she thinks she had low self-esteem, that she got married because she did not think anybody else would have her.

'I don't think I grew up with deprivation,' she says. 'I remember a beautiful white frilly dress, with a red ribbon ... also a dress with little yellow flowers, red slippers with little ears and bells, my little pram and the pedal car.'

Karen did not leave. She did not recognise what was happening to her as family violence. Her perception of family violence was, 'you get belted every night. Your husband is an alcoholic. I understood the emotional component, but not the finances.' It was only after the end of her 20-year marriage, one of her friends told her she had suffered economic abuse, that she had experienced family violence.

Her story is one of empowering herself emotionally and financially through education, while remaining married. One of her friends, a nurse, paid for her to attend a Christian course. She says, 'It cost $300 for a week, which was a lot of money then. I read a book "Love is a decision."' When she read the back page, she felt more empowered, more willing to stand up.

Her husband shirtfronted her 12-year-old daughter, as if to stand over her. He hit her when she was 15. Karen told him it was really intimidating. Karen began seriously thinking of leaving.

By this time, she was studying for a music degree part time, 1994 to 2000. Her maternal grandfather's money meant for her mother, came to her. Her husband did not really know how much she received. She would go from regional Victoria to Melbourne for a day or two a week, pay her friends $8 a night to look after her two children, and then work on her assignments and do the piano tuitions. This degree enabled her to teach the higher-grade students at school.

The exit from her marriage came not because of his lack of provision, his affairs, or his violence. Seeing the table in the lounge full of papers, she suggested they rent another house. He could use the present one for his office. She says, 'He threw the laptop like a frisbee across the room and threw the papers,' and said they could divorce. They did. They had a property settlement in 1998, divorced in 1999, 20 years after marriage, but were still sharing the same bed till 2000. She took the kids away for Easter in 2000. When 'we came home he had moved out.'

She got 55 per cent of the house for her children were just 17 and 18. She had to pay off his $10,000 debt. He paid $5 a month for the children. By this time, she was teaching music in two schools.

Karen's husband committed suicide shortly after. He had threatened suicide earlier, but they had not received or sought help. The police came to the door on a Friday night asking if the father was there. There had been a missing person report for he was expected at a barbeque in Melbourne. She told the police he had been there two days earlier, for a 10-minute visit to his children.

On Saturday at 10 am the police found his van wedged into the front of a tree. Apparently, he had walked into the bush and drank Draino. They found him in the middle of the bush, curled up, and took him to the Royal Melbourne where they induced a coma.

Karen and the children went to see him on Sunday and sat with him. They went again on Thursday. On Friday night they heard he had died. Karen went to the church to tell her son who was playing drums. They stood there with their arms around each other. Her son went to university, six weeks after his father's suicide to do graphic design. None of them got counselling.

In 2003, she started her psychology course then her Masters. Her children had to guarantee the loan for her books. She says there was 'one profound moment in 2005 in the health psychology class, when the lecturer was speaking of the suicide statistics for 2000, and I thought 'my husband is one of those.'

She is a psychologist now, but still into piano teaching. Even now, when she buys a new blouse, she remarks on it. She can now spend up to a $100 a week on groceries. She strategises her use of money. She bought an almost new Honda Civic. When it was standing outside in the rain, she thought it looked just like the advertisements.

She and the children bought a house in the outer east of Melbourne. The children helped with the deposit, but she will take care of the payments. She is now thinking of their inheritance as she considers what to do with their house in regional Victoria.

Though there were tears during the two hours we spoke, Karen knows she is in a good place. She has friends, family, a good relationship with her children, work she talks about with pleasure, and financial independence.

Neither of the children married. Karen's daughter earns twice as much as Karen does, and is generous. She shops so much that Karen calls her Ms Melbourne. She wonders whether it is because she had to go in her trackies to university because there was no money for new clothes.

Karen says her son is a 'good saver. He can spin a dollar like his mother.' He said, last year was the first year he did not remember the anniversary of his father's suicide. This was 16 years ago. Karen offered him $4,000 at Christmas to have his teeth fixed as she could not afford it when he was 16. He said, he has gotten used to them.

Now that he has a girlfriend, he worries whether he is like his father. Karen reassures him.

Karen says, having talked of her life with friends, she is able to look at her husband with a different lens. She can say, maybe he did come from a family with a background of family violence. She and her children make sure they talk of their problems and uncomfortable subjects, such as family violence, so that the cycle is not repeated.

As Karen gets up to leave, I tell her, she survived. She gives me a hug and says, 'Not survived Supriya, empowered.'

7 Asha

'You now belong to my family and your money is mine'

Introduction

I met Asha[1] at an Indian networking dinner. The conversation soon went to personal matters. Asha said she was waiting for her divorce to come through, and that money and remittances were part of the story. We sat at the table long after most of the others had left. The conversation continued as we walked to the tram stop.

When I began researching economic abuse, Asha came to my office after work. She spoke of herself, her family and money in her marriage for two and a half hours over crackers, cheese, and dips.

Asha, 32, is a software developer, born in India. She comes from a large extended family and is one of two daughters. Her dream was to be a pilot in the Indian Air Force. While doing her Bachelor of Computer Science, she took flying lessons. She says she was rebellious, independent, and determined. But when she needed spectacles, that was the end of her dream of becoming a pilot. She then followed her second passion of computer engineering.

Asha came to Melbourne in 2007 to do her graduate degree in software engineering. She chose Melbourne, partly because as a child she had heard her father talk of Australia, and how he had hoped to settle in Australia. He had to look after his parents, so he stayed in India. She remembers her father always joked, 'that he will export his eldest daughter to Australia.'

Her father borrowed against his shares to finance her study with the understanding she will repay the loan once she started working. Three months after she arrived, she landed a part time job as a Java

---

1 The names are pseudonyms. Some details have been generalised to ensure confidentiality.

DOI: 10.4324/9781003178606-7

programmer. It did not pay much but it led her to other consultancies and work. In 2009, instead of flying, she was developing air traffic management systems. Four years later, she moved to a large company as a lead business analyst, after having negotiated equal pay.

Asha was successful and focussed. Three years after she came to Melbourne, she met Aman who was also from India, though from a different region and religion. He was in hospitality and earned less than her but had dreams of setting up his own restaurant. They dated for six months.

Her parents were not enthusiastic about him. Later, she thought she should have respected her own intuition that they were not a good fit. She should have interacted more with his family before marriage for she had seen them only for two days before the wedding. During those two days, she did not figure out the cultural differences.

> I was raised independently where women are given their due respect ... Simple things like if my father is driving the car, or if we're going out somewhere, usually my mother would sit next to him and my uncle and my aunt would sit behind, if the four of them are going... In his [her husband's] family, the brother and the husband would sit in the front and the women took the back seat.

Asha thought she had spoken openly about money with Aman. She had explained her financial responsibilities to her family. But her relationship was over in less than two years after Asha experienced economic, physical and emotional abuse.

Asha met three other women from South Asia, where the woman was the chief earner but did not control the money. Like her, they were seeking help because of family violence. She says she felt, 'I'm not the only idiot.'

She says when she experienced emotional, physical, and economic abuse, she did think she was an idiot. She says, '... your self-esteem is low so you ... analyse yourself and then you over-analyse yourself and then you blame yourself for the situation.' Looking back, she thinks she should have been more compassionate with herself.

Being a 'good daughter' and a partner in marriage

When Asha began a full-time job, she sent her father $1000[2] a month to repay the loan to keep her side of the bargain. Her father had not asked for the money. She later learnt he had already repaid the loan, but he

---

2   The money is in Australian dollars, unless stated otherwise.

accepted the money she sent. After she had repaid the loan, her father had a stroke. For a while he could not walk or talk. Her mother became his full-time carer. Asha continued to send the $1000 home, to pay for the physiotherapist, the speech therapist, and the Kerala-style masseur.

Asha told Aman before getting married 'I have this financial responsibility ... my father is paralysed, and I need to send this money to him every month. And if you have any issues with this ... we should reconsider getting married.'

Asha and her husband discussed the management and control of their money in their marriage. 'He wanted me to give my salary to him and then he manages all the finances. I said, "No, I can put a percentage of my salary towards a joint account."'

They had put an equal amount towards the deposit for their home. Each agreed to put $2000 into a joint account each month and keep the rest of their money separate. She would send the $1000 from her own money and save the rest. She said, 'he can do whatever he wants to do from ... whatever is remaining from his salary. I had to look after my parents.'

Both agreements fell apart two months after they were married. Aman did not want her to send money home. She says Aman was unhappy 'that I was supporting my parents ... I didn't see it was wrong in any way. I was supporting the expenses here, but I had to support my parents as well and that was one of the major issues.'

Soon after they married, Aman did not put his full $2000 into the joint account. Sometimes he would put $500 into it, leaving her to put in her $2000 in the joint account and be responsible for the monthly $2000 towards the mortgage. Aman accused Asha of not putting in her full share. Although she was the main earner and contributing more, he criticised her for spending $2 on a packet of spicy pappadum. He said he could get it for less in another suburb.

She says, 'It didn't make sense ... it was a matter of control.' Asha explains,

> It was control of money. It was being in control whether it is money or any situation. It started with, 'Why are you sending this money to your father? You are married to me ... so you should be giving all your money to me. You are now [a member] of my family.'

It was also a conflict in their ideas of the gender of money. Asha had grown up thinking she would not live a sequestered life like her mother, when it came to money. She sought – and her parents funded – the best education she could have. So, she also accepted the responsibilities of care for her parents by sending money home.

Her husband, Aman, continued to think that Asha's money belonged to him and his family. Though she explained her perspective, his template of money continued to be traditional.

He queried her sending money to her parents. He also questioned why she was worshipping her gods instead of his. 'You are now from my family. You are not from your family.' He wanted her to go to his temple and eat chapattis rather than rice. He told her cooking rice is behaving like a beggar.

Six months into the marriage, Aman kicked Asha in her stomach. This is when she breaks down telling her story. She says, 'I could take the emotional abuse, I could take the verbal abuse, but I could not comprehend a man beating me.' She adds,

> That's when I realised [it was] the whole cycle of abuse and the violence that the websites talk about.... My husband's fine for five days. Then he finds a fault. Then he reprimands me. Then he blames the victim for abusing or creating this situation. And then he apologises, and then again, he goes into the fault-finding cycle.... He did not have any compassion; he didn't have any empathy and he was very controlling.... It was clear to me to just get divorced, settle the property, and move away from that situation.

At first, she did not tell her parents what was happening to her. Her father was ill and her mother had enough on her plate. Later she told her mother about the emotional abuse and how her husband said only beggars eat rice. Her mother told her to stop cooking rice, showing her ways of avoiding conflict.

Asha then told her father's good friend in India. He said the first year is difficult, for the woman has to adapt to a different family. Asha told her husband's brother of her husband's physical abuse, but he only said he would talk to his brother. The abuse continued.

When she finally told her father, he was blunt. He said, 'Get out or get beaten.' He was angry with his friend for having advised her otherwise.

Asha got out of her marriage.

Surviving family violence

Asha remained financially sustainable though she did not get half the equity of the home. She got $32,000 instead of $50,000. He got more. But she decided she needed her peace of mind and got out. She bought a unit in the south-west, moved back to live in the city, and is now focussed on building up her investments.

Reflecting on the time after her marriage, she says she is grateful for her friends, colleagues, and mentors who stood by her. She also has the ability to logically analyse what happened during the marriage. She even put it in an excel sheet, laughing and saying, she is an engineer after all.

She says she had grown up in a family that nurtured freedom. Her grandparents and father were entrepreneurs and supported their children. She had not thought someone else would look after her financially. She had invested in her education and work experience. Asha says,

> My parents always supported me in whatever decisions I made, whether it was flying or coming to Australia. I am the eldest and I am like the trendsetter at home in every way – with the divorce as well now.

She had grown up with spirituality. Her grandmother would teach her Sanskrit *slokas* when walking her to nursery school. She learnt Sanskrit before any other language. After Asha's marriage ended, she found solace with a spiritual teacher. Asha says,

> I always thank God for my situation. He has always placed these beautiful souls, beautiful people in my life at certain ... milestones in my life ... They have come and delivered this message to me in some way or the other, and I have been able to steer myself through the rough waters.

Asha ends the conversation saying, 'I want to thank you for giving me this opportunity to speak about myself, and hopefully people can get something out of it.'

8 Chitra

He and his family abused her because she did not behave 'like a good wife'

Introduction

Chitra[1] got in touch with the researchers through social media. She wanted to tell her story of family violence. When I went after work to interview her, I found Chitra's mother and brother were staying with her in her rented unit. Chitra's mother had cooked dinner and after dinner we started the recorded interview. We spoke in Hindi, Punjabi and English.

Chitra, 29, was a health professional in India when she agreed to an arranged marriage. She comes from a family of professionals. Her mother is a single parent and has taken care of the family through difficult times.

Chitra's mother says the boy's side pursued the arranged marriage. She knew them because a woman from their kinship network was married to one of their relatives. The boy's parents said they wanted their son to marry an educated girl. There was no demand for dowry. However, as the wedding came closer, the boy's family said they wanted the best hospitality possible for the boy's family and friends. Chitra's maternal grandmother gave Chitra jewellery as part of her dowry. The family also gave gold sets to the mother-in-law and sisters-in-law. Rings were given to the father, brother, and brother-in-law.

The emotional, physical, and economic abuse made her doubt herself

The honeymoon grooming period was short. She arrived in Australia in 2012 on a spouse visa to join her husband's joint family. She wrote,

---

[1] The names are pseudonyms. Some details have been generalised to ensure confidentiality.

DOI: 10.4324/9781003178606-8

'I loved my husband, and I was very happy to be finally with him. I looked forward to a happy life with the people who would now be my family for the rest of my life.'

Early in the marriage, Chitra's husband did not talk to her at all. She says,

> He would leave for his work in the morning and on returning home, he would not even say, 'Hi' to me. He ignored me to a great extent. I asked him the reason. He said that his family will not like it if he talked to me. From the very first day, my husband was not committed to our relationship. He used to say that he belonged to his family and he will never be mine. This showed in his behaviour for he only came to the room to sleep. This made me feel so lonely and ignored. I had no one in this country. Just him. But he did not seem to understand.

Within the first year in Australia, her husband told her she talked too much. He insulted her in front of his family. There were continual remarks she had not brought enough into the marriage. They said they had done her a favour for no one else would have married her. Her mother-in-law said Chitra was not good enough for her son, although they had chosen her.

His family laughed at her, saying she was a liar, that she was from a poor family unlike the older daughter-in-law, and she was pretending to be ill. They did not let her go to the doctor saying she was just trying to avoid doing the household chores. The other daughter-in-law, however, went shopping and met with relatives and friends. It was Chitra who was expected to stay at home and do the household chores. 'There were always some snide remarks,' Chitra says. 'I started to lose belief in myself and lost my self-esteem. I started to believe in the words I was hearing.'

Chitra's husband was suspicious of her talking to anyone, including her family. The doctor's receptionist told Chitra her husband had come to check whether she really had an appointment with the doctor.

Chitra's in-laws would read her personal emails and messages to her family, without her consent, when she was not around. She says, 'I had no privacy. The whole family knew all the time what I was doing and talking to others.' They made her feel like a 'slave.' Chitra was told she could not sit, stand or talk properly. She says, 'They never let me go out. And then they used to say, "I have no friends. I don't get along with anybody."' They did not allow her to drive though she had an Indian driving licence and had driven interstate in India.

She did not talk to the neighbours for she thought what was happening to her was a personal matter. She also did not feel she could. Her husband and his family felt so strong. It was as if 'They were correct always. Only you are wrong. How can all of us be wrong? Since you are not getting along with any person and have no friends, only you can be wrong.'

There was a malicious cruelty in this abuse. Chitra's husband said, see how I disturb your mother. He called her at 2.30 am Indian time to say her daughter is troubling them. The family threatened they would have Chitra deported from Australia because she was only on a spousal visa.

Soon, Chitra's husband started hitting her when she asked him for anything. She says,

> His mother, brother and his sister would ask him to keep me under control and would ask him to slap me if I resented anything. My mother-in-law used to say to my husband that if he listened to me, then their family would leave him.... She also used to say that my husband should not listen to me because I belonged to a poor family and girls like me are taught to ... break down joint families.

Chitra's husband and his brother, encouraged by their mother, beat Chitra. Her husband's brother would tell Chitra's husband, 'Hit her and make her quiet.' Her mother-in-law told her son, 'If you support her, get out of my house.' Her husband blamed Chitra, saying, he wouldn't hit her if she behaved 'like a good wife.'

Chitra says,

> I tried my best all the time to be a good wife and do whatever he wanted me to do. I was so scared all the time that I was so careful about what I was saying, because anything I said or did, they would start scolding me. I was so scared to tell this to anyone because they always made me believe that I was the wrong one. I had lost trust in myself.

They sabotaged her ability to engage in her profession for they did not allow her to qualify so that she could continue her work as a health professional. Her husband said she should concentrate on household chores. Her sister-in-law said she was too dumb to qualify.

Her mother-in-law took away Chitra's jewellery, saying it was not safe to keep it at home. It was kept in her brother-in-law's bank locker.

A year after Chitra arrived in Australia, she began working, though not as a health professional. Her husband said they should open a joint account for it would help with the visa for permanent residence. The joint account only held her earnings. Chitra says,

> When my salary started coming, I wasn't checking my account regularly. I once checked my account, and it had a certain amount of money. I thought that's okay, that's what must have been there. The next time when I checked, it was still the same. I asked him, 'My bank amount is not increasing. Is my salary coming or not?' He said that he withdraws that amount. I had no idea that he was going to take my money. I told him, 'At least leave some amount for me too, for my personal needs.' He said, 'Oh you want to spend money now.'

She hoped to save to pay the fees to qualify for her work as a health professional. However, her husband always wanted the money for something else. It was her mother's intervention, which made it possible for her to partially qualify.

The day after Chitra passed her first exam to continue her professional work in Australia, her husband beat her 'mercilessly.' She tried to escape but her husband's brother and his wife pulled her back. She then ran out again, straight to the police station, fearing for her life.

When she left, there was no money in her joint account. It was only during this interview, she found she was also entangled in 'coercive debt' through a directorship in the joint family business and a loan. Within three years her marriage was over.

Chitra seeks help

Chitra told her mother what was happening to her in Australia after three or four violent episodes. This was within the first year of her stay in Australia. Her mother told her to be patient. She said, 'Everything will be alright. In the beginning, it is always difficult.' But the barbs continued.

Chitra would sit at the train station on her way back home and call her mother. She would cry because she was lonely. She often rang the Domestic Violence helpline. She was advised to go to the police. When she finally went to the police after her husband and his family beat her, they asked her for a statement so they could press for an Apprehended Violence Order (AVO). Thinking she did not want to put her husband in trouble, she said she would give the statement later. The Help Line told her she had put herself in a tight spot and advised her to go to the hospital.

The hospital gave her a report. She stayed there the night and went back to the police the next day to give a statement and ask for an AVO. As no refuge was available over the weekend she went to stay with a friend from work. The third day she went into the refuge and felt safe.

She stayed at the refuge for six months. She had counselling, which is still continuing over the phone. She got her permanent residence. After six months at the refuge, she moved interstate to stay for six months with extended family. Chitra says, 'they supported me quite a lot.'

She felt she was strung in the middle. She did not want to go back to her husband and his family. But she 'was not ready to take any action against him. I was not ready because maybe I still loved him.' There was no resolution. Her husband's brother went to India and spoke with Chitra's grandparents. The mediator said, 'If the children are not getting along well, return the girl's things.' Chitra's brother-in-law said, 'We have nothing. She has taken away everything, even our thick bangles and rings.'

At the time of the interview, Chitra had received a notice for divorce. This trashed her hopes that she and her husband could sort something out, independent of his family. Chitra says, 'If someone asks me to stay with them, I don't think that I have the capacity now. I can't suffer all that again because I have been traumatised to an extent that I can't tolerate it anymore.' All those hopes and fears became theoretical with the notice for divorce.

The financial settlement was still to be negotiated. The advice she has had is that she is not entitled to much, for the marriage was so short. But she needed to resolve the matter of coerced debt.

It was difficult for her to get help from non-governmental organisations (NGOs) dealing with family violence. She was no longer in crisis and so not a priority. The one-stop police hub did not work for her. Financial counsellors did not help. She was employed and could not get legal aid. But she had little money for private lawyers, for she had left her marriage with none.

This is the time she wanted somebody to hold her hand. In the three weeks after the interview in mid-2016, I counted 25 SMS and two telephone calls between her and I. It was as if she had fallen through the cracks of the family violence support system. In the end, she found help with a multicultural NGO.

Chitra is living independently though income security is still precarious. She has family support, but the road ahead is challenging.

9 Prema

He married her to get permanent residence

Introduction: Prema migrated to Australia to escape the 'normal' family violence in her family

Prema,[1] 36, came to Australia to escape the family violence she saw in her family and around her in India. Her story is one of great enterprise in settling down and becoming resilient in Australia as a skilled migrant. Pressured by her family, she agreed to marry a man who was marrying her because she had permanent residence (PR). After a short period of grooming, he subjected Prema to horrific physical, emotional, reproductive, and economic abuse.

Just before I interviewed her in 2017, Prema had stood before an audience and told her story as a family violence survivor. This is where I first saw her.

Prema is from a regional city in Punjab. Her father had a vegetable shop near their home. There was enough money to eat, but he did not pay for her education. Her father thought, 'Boys are assets and girls are liabilities.' He had three 'liabilities.' He was angry. He would get them married early, so there was no point in educating them. Her brother – the elder of two – was also 'very anti-women.'

They lived in a joint family household where the house belonged to her paternal grandfather. Prema was close to him and her grandmother. At one time her father's younger brothers and their families also lived there.

Prema's father drank a lot and beat her mother. His brother beat his wife. Her paternal grandfather did not beat his wife. Yet the grandfather and grandmother did not support the daughters-in-law. Domestic

---

1 The names are pseudonyms. Some details have been generalised to ensure confidentiality.

DOI: 10.4324/9781003178606-9

violence, that is physical violence, was 'normal' Prema says, 'Mummy never told anyone, but everybody knew that this is what happens in India. Nothing new. I thought it was normal but I didn't want that to be normal in my life.'

When she was six or seven years old, she saw her father 'holding a sword in his hand as if he would kill my mother. We were hiding ... That incident is still very fresh in my mind ... It was that bad.'

Her parents fought all the time. Prema says,

> That's why I wanted to run away from there. I felt that when I marry tomorrow, the same thing will happen with me. So I better run away to a country where nothing of this sort happens ... If I become something tomorrow, nobody would dare misbehave with me.

She thought family violence only happened in India.

Prema had to fight her father and brother to study till Year 10 and then to do a Bachelor of Education (B.Ed.). Her mother supported her, though she only had two years of schooling. But her mother had no money in hand and her grandparents did not contribute. The school principal waived Prema's fees for Year 10 for she was a very bright student. She got 89 per cent in her Year 10 exams and came first in the district. After that, she was awarded a scholarship till Year 12. Her photograph was in the newspaper. Her father's younger brother said, she had brightened the name of the family.

She did her BA and B.Ed. supporting herself with tuitions. She used to go to the students' homes for she did not want her father to know. After graduating, she taught in school. She also started a tuition centre of her own, charging a student Rs 450 a month. She had six or seven groups of seven students a day. With this money she helped educate her youngest sister in India and got her a scooter. Her sister was able to do what Prema never was able to do, like going to a restaurant. Now she is a major support for Prema.

The money from her teaching and Provident Fund helped her pay for the move to Australia. Prema came to Australia in 2005, as a skilled migrant with PR. She chose Australia over Canada because the fee was lower. After paying the Rs 60,000 fee and Rs 15,000 to the agent, she came with $450[2] to Australia. Her mother's sister bought her the ticket. She told her father about her plans for Australia only when the

---

2   The money is in Australian dollars.

PR card arrived after a few months. Her mother knew about it for she 'always sided' with Prema.

When she left for Australia, she was pressured to get married. People asked 'Who sends a single girl overseas?' But the visa said she had to come as a single person and not with her husband. She also did not want to get married. A cousin suggested that now that her passport has a PR stamp, she could sell it for Rs 400,000–500,000. But Prema left. She wore her first pair of jeans to go to the airport, for one of her friends had said, 'Nobody wears Indian clothes in Australia.'

Becomes self-reliant in Australia, then marries under pressure

In Australia, Prema first stayed with her aunt's friend for 15–20 days. After 15 days she found a job as a kitchen hand. It was cash in hand, $8 an hour. Then she coached a Year 12 student for two to three days for his exam. His father was a supervisor in a factory- which packed laptops. He got her registered with the factory and she started working there at $27 an hour. She also gave tuitions for eight to nine months.

She then moved interstate, had her teaching qualifications registered and worked as a casual teacher for three years. She got tired of not having a permanent job and moved to customer service. For a while, she was working a full-time job together with another casual job.

She was single for five years in Australia and financially self-sufficient. In 2010, her maternal uncle's sister-in-law knew of a boy who was an international student in Queensland. His visa was expiring soon. He had been in an accident and had a brain injury and no job. It was as if Prema was a 'goat for slaughter.' There was enormous pressure. She kept resisting. The man came to Victoria to see her. He was six years younger and childish. She kept saying no, and her family said, 'We are here.'

When she went back to India, the questions were why she was not married. Her father and brothers yelled that her not being married is bringing them shame. Even if she had to marry a *rickshawala*, she had to get married. She was nearly 30 years old.

She got married.

The violence starts early

The first year was good, though she knew, 'He was getting married to my passport, my PR card.' Even his papers for education in Australia were fake. He only had a Year 12 education.

They had a daughter. His mother was angry for the religious teacher she believed in, had said they would have a son. In her six-year marriage, they made her abort four children.

Her husband hit her, slapped her. She thought it was because of his brain injury. She felt if she went to the police, she would lose her family in India. She did not tell her mother. His family was threatening her family in India.

Three years after getting married, he poured drain cleaner down her throat to kill her. She showed me serrations on her neck going right down her stomach. Her stomach had to be joined to the oesophagus. Her gut leaks and she has a hard time eating. She has gained a few of the 13 kgs she lost.

Her husband threatened he would kill their daughter, if she told the police about the drain cleaner. So, she told the police she had tried to commit suicide. When she did tell the police of the violence, he had already destroyed the bottle. There was no proof. He was never charged.

Prema was the main earner. She paid the rent and the mortgage. Her money went into a separate account. She gave him money to set up a business. The money from the business was supposed to go into a joint account. But he gambled $35,000 within six months.

Prema also supported and coached her husband for jobs. She taught him how to speak better English. For a while he worked, and his salary went into the joint account. But for two years he did not work. This was partly so his case for compensation for the accident would be stronger.

When he finally got his compensation of $200,000 five years after marriage, he did not tell her and took it all to India. She only found out when she went to India. When she remonstrated that the money was for him to establish a business, her mother-in-law said, if she makes trouble they will burn her.

Prema returned to Australia and was pregnant again. His sister came from India bringing abortion pills. Prema would not have them. Her mother also said, 'Don't listen to him, we will support you.'

Her husband threatened to divorce her if she did not have the abortion. Prema told him to go ahead with the divorce. He fixed her appointment for an abortion the next morning. He asked her to take off her earrings and the *mangalsutra*, the black bead and gold necklace that symbolises marriage. Prema refused to go. She cried, saying it was affecting her psychologically that she was killing unborn babies.

Her husband and his sister went out. Prema and her daughter were at the library. They called to find out where she was. Prema went back and started cooking. She felt something was different. Their clothes had gone. Her husband and his sister stole all her jewellery and went to India.

She reported this to the police, but they said it was a civil case.

In the end, she could not keep the child. Her family did not come to Australia to help her. Prema left her daughter with her married sister's in-laws in India for two months so that she could get herself together. But her daughter became quiet and was depressed.

Prema did not know how she could look after two children. She was in bad health with a leaky gut syndrome. She had no car. Prema herself had sunk into depression and blamed herself for the divorce. She hardly slept. At work she would cry. She feared she was going mad.

She aborted the child. She got a car, learnt to drive and then went to India to get her daughter.

Surviving family violence

Prema has a part time job at $37 an hour at night and at times a casual one in the morning. Her daughter goes to stay with a 'day care' family during the night. Prema is about to finish two diplomas relating to children and community services. She hopes these will enable her to be a trainer.

Prema has no family in Australia. She has a friend, she met at her workplace 10 years ago. This is an Indian woman and her best friend. Other than this one person, Prema does not tell anyone about her problems. She has been supported at work. Her managers helped when she went from being the best customer service officer to one who would start crying and remain silent. They did not ask her to leave. They know some of her story, but she has not told them the details. Her neighbour and his wife, also Indian, help her sometimes.

She does not tell anyone in the Sikh or Hindu temple. She does not want anyone pitying her. She is using support organisations. When the judge in the Family Court found she had no family, the judge referred her to InTouch, a multicultural centre against family violence. There she got to know some South Asian women who had also suffered family violence. When it was her daughter's birthday, she called them all for a party.

She has legal help from the Family Law Assistance Program (FLAP), but the quality of the help depends on the student allocated to her. Through FLAP she gets a barrister for the day for $1500, though she prepares the paperwork herself. She sees herself as self-represented, though technically she is represented.

She goes for counselling to Drummond St. Services. Her experience of marriage and family violence left her with 'zero confidence.' She used to remain quiet. Now at least she can communicate. She also works with another Indian non-governmental organisation (NGO) to help women who are experiencing family violence. She got to know the woman heading this NGO, for her friend had asked her to help Prema when she was ill and pregnant.

The trauma goes deep. Prema blames herself for the divorce. She asks, 'What will I tell my daughter? I am the one to blame for what happened. I have snatched her father from her.'

She says,

> I was a rebel, but I always wanted to settle in life. I wanted a proper family with the man, woman and children living happily. (I thought) that one day when I marry, nobody will hit me ... I will do all the best things that I can do in life. So, I was always giving my 100 per cent, like going to the job, making food at home, cleaning up the house, whatever I could do as a woman.

She cries, wondering why this happened to her. She thought divorce was a swear word. Why wasn't a normal husband in her destiny? She asks herself what wrong did she do that so many terrible things have happened to her. 'I did not think I would be divorced. I thought it would be fine one day.'

Though she explicitly did not want family violence, during her marriage she began to see family violence as normal. So what if your husband hits you? She says,

> Two days before he left, I gave a knife in his hand and told him to cut me. I will not say a word. I am not bothered since you are my husband.... I felt that my life without him would be nothing. Even today, I feel as if Prema has died. Only my daughter's mother is alive.... I still have a soft corner for him. He is my husband, he is everything for me. That's how I was brought up.

Prema's life now revolves around her six-year-old daughter. She is slowly gaining in confidence. She says, 'I am making a masterpiece. Maybe that is the best thing that I will be able to contribute to the world. My daughter makes friends. Everybody praises her.' Prema says her daughter is still young, but she is her counsellor. Prema says, 'Some time ago, she said, "Beautiful woman!" I said, "I am not beautiful." She said, "Everybody is beautiful in their own way. So, you are beautiful. Remember that."'

Later, when we go to McDonald, one of the jokes she shares with her daughter is 'Mama will slap you.' To which her daughter mimicking a film song says, 'I am not scared of your slap. I am only scared of your love.'

Prema worries she may lose her. She says, the Family Court does not consider family violence when deciding custody and financial settlement. The father has two hours supervised access, but the daughter does not want to see him. She is scared. Her daughter has been put on Airport watch. They joke whether they can go by car to London, but think they will go to Sydney one day.

Her ex-husband's lawyer paints her as being mentally unstable and not fit to be a mother. At the same time, he says, Prema earns too much. Prema says to him, 'I can't be both.' Prema is determined her daughter will not suffer family violence. She says, 'I had no support. I will stand by her side. Let anybody touch her; I'll kill that person.'

Getting back in touch with Prema for this story, I learn she began working as a trainer and assessor in 2017. She was diagnosed with breast cancer in April 2019. Many friends came to help when she was undergoing chemotherapy. She says, 'I used to live the life of a victim. So, I always kept quiet and tolerated everything. But no more. I will live the life of a hero who will be a guiding star for her daughter.' She adds, 'I am a lesson for others that you need to put yourself before everyone in the world.'

10 Betty

After he died she recognised it as economic abuse

Betty's husband did not provide

Betty,[1] 66, was married to Brad for 37 years. I met her through my personal network six years after her husband died. We sit in Betty's three-bedroom unit where she tells her story over tea and cake. Betty could not understand how her husband never had money on him, why he did not give her housekeeping, never paid the bills and drove her to attempt suicide.

Her husband, Brad, would give her housekeeping one month and then say there is no more money. Brad was short of money even on their honeymoon.

> He had plenty of money or seemed to have plenty of money ... I saw this Wedgwood dinner set that I wanted to buy. He wrote out a cheque. When we got back to where we were staying, he said 'I don't think I've got enough money in that account.' I remember thinking, well why did you write a cheque if you haven't got money in the account? So I went back to the man with my cheque. I didn't think anything of it. And really, it was downhill from there.

When they got married, Brad owned a hotel. Soon Betty had two children and was not in paid work. One day she rang her dentist, and they said, 'No, we're not taking you anymore because you won't pay your bill.' She did not even see the bill. Though it was addressed to her, Brad just put it where he put all the other bills. She says, 'I didn't go to that dentist anymore and I remember being really upset about that.'

---

1 The names are pseudonyms. The details have been generalised to ensure confidentiality.

DOI: 10.4324/9781003178606-10

Brad ended up losing the hotel. Money was tight. Betty said, she and the children went away one school holidays. When they came back, the locks on their rental place had been changed. She says,

> I had to go over to the phone box and ring Brad and say, 'I can't get in,' and he went off and paid it. But it was always this last-minute stuff. Another time it was Easter Sunday and I opened the door, and this man was standing there saying, 'I want the rent, like, yesterday.'

When her third child was three months old, Betty went to work as a secretary. She says,

> I just thought, 'I can't deal with this anymore.' I'd had the Sheriff come. He came in and hung labels on my washing machine and television ... I was crying ... The sheriff said he was going to have a public auction on our lawn.

When Betty told Brad about the sheriff, he 'did this big sigh and said, "You just can't cope can you?"'

Betty would start to shake when the doorbell rang, or when somebody asked whether she was married to Brad. She was nervous that Brad owed them money.

They lived on the money she earned as a secretary. She paid the bills. She was the one who put food on the table. She was exhausted and got pleurisy in the first two years after working.

She had saved $3,000.[2] They put a deposit on a house in regional Victoria. Her husband was supposed to pay the mortgage.

> Within about 18 months I had a fellow at the door issuing us with a warrant – we had to get out of the premises within 14 days because we were six months in arrears or something. So I went straight over to the Building Society and I just dealt with these things and I kept dealing with them. I was always behind the eight ball.

He would say to her without giving any reason, that he couldn't give her housekeeping this pay. She says one Easter she had invited the family to lunch. Brad loved the garden and bought pansies and other things in long narrow boxes. On Saturday, Betty asked Brad for money

---

2 The money is in Australian dollars.

to buy lamb and chicken. He told her, 'You can't. I've spent it all on the flowers.' Betty cried. She doesn't remember what she did for Easter lunch.

She began to pay the mortgage and then the parking fines started. She says,

> They'd be $65 and then he'd ignore them, and then they'd go to $120, and then they'd end up at the magistrates' court, and they'd be $260. One day I rang one of the courts and I asked, 'Exactly how much does he owe?' because I was paying them out of my pay all of the time. And he said, 'Hang on a minute' and he said, '$9000.'

It was just a constant lack of money. He would say, '"I am going to book us a trip to Singapore for the family." I'd say "Brad, who's paying for it?" I was always the wicked witch of the West saying, "We can't afford it, you can't do this."'

She constantly worried about money. Her two sons and one daughter went to Catholic schools, but she was still paying their fees at $50 a month, even when they were two years into university. Her daughter told her that her brother had a hole in his shoe. She took him to buy shoes, but he said his shoes felt warm.

She thinks their constant wrangling led to her daughter suffering anorexia and bulimia, and years of distance between her and Betty. But her husband never apologised to Betty. Instead, he told her and the children that the fault lay with Betty, that she was too controlling and obsessive about money. He would say, 'I've done nothing wrong.' In one argument, she hit him, and after that he said he was a victim of domestic violence.

She was brittle with stress. The despair just became too much. Betty says, 'I just couldn't keep coping with it. It was so demoralising because the harder I worked the less I got.' They separated many times, but she always relented and had him back. She says,

> He was fun. And he was smart. Everybody loved him. A friend of mine was here the other night and she said, 'People were just drawn to him.' In one of my rows with him over money, I told Brad 'I think you're a con man.' Because con men are very presentable, aren't they? They get people in.

In one period of separation, when he was 50, he withdrew his super and put it in a winery. It was not there 18 months later. 'The German couple could see him coming' Betty says.

Once when the stress in her marriage became too much to bear, Betty went back home. Betty's mother had died when Betty was 34. Betty had never gotten along with her father. Her father said, 'I always knew you were housing commission material,' that she was a failure. Betty says she always felt the black sheep of the family. He was drinking and so rude to her one day that she lunged at him holding his head over a sink. Then she rang her sister and said, 'I nearly killed Dad today.' When Brad said, 'Let's get back together' Betty says, 'I ran into his arms because Dad didn't want me. I was an embarrassment.'

Brought up as an Irish Catholic she could not bring herself to leave the marriage, even though she cried every day. Her sister had also told her a single mother would find it difficult to bring up boys. She attempted suicide three times. She threw a rope over a beam in the shed once. Another time she stuck a vacuum cleaner in the car until she began to think of her kids.

Though Betty's father was not supportive, she is close to her older sister who listened and gave her treats and gifts. Her brother bought her a fare to Europe when her daughter was sick there. She was able to talk openly to friends and colleagues.

Betty's husband was earning $62,000 a year when he died. Betty was 60 at the time and had been retrenched and so was working part time for $28,000. Brad always paid his membership fees for the Melbourne Cricket Club. He had long lunches with drinks, though one of his friends said it was his friends who were often left with the bill.

He always had a new car. When his car needed a big service, he didn't have the money so he'd trade it in and get another one. Betty says, 'I couldn't stop him.' Two weeks before Brad died when he was 67, he said, 'Let's go to Ireland.' Betty asked who was paying for the tickets. He went to Ireland and maxed out his credit cards.

Betty does not know what led to her husband's financial mismanagement. It was not all due to gambling for they found tickets, which were for $4. She thinks his parents spoilt him. They did not charge him board. He never returned what he borrowed. She once spoke to her mother-in-law whom she liked very much about their money troubles. But her mother-in-law looked away in the distance.

Brad's approach to money contrasted with the way Betty had been brought up. Though her parents never talked about money, Betty says her mother used to say, '"Your father has never missed a housekeeping payment,"' and he never did. And I used to think "What's so special about that?" But Betty's mother never knew what he earned. There was no sharing. Betty thinks this was very much how Irish men dealt with money. They 'sort of ruled the roost.'

Betty's mother had her own money and bank account. She had inherited money from her mother and so had bought the house with cash 300 pounds. She used to say, 'Your father has never bought me a dress.' Anything she ever wanted she bought herself out of her own money. They were comfortable. They had a car and a phone. Betty says, 'We only went on camping holidays, but we were comfortable.'

Betty grew up being prudent with money. She says, 'When I first went to work at 17, I was earning 9 pounds 10 a week. Mum said, "Put 5 pounds away" and I did. And I always have. The kids have always laughed and said, "Mum's always got something in spare."'

Betty, like her mother, always had her own money and bank account. She says,

> I never even thought to join a bank account with him, and I wouldn't have. I had my own bank card and everything. But he was supposed to give me housekeeping. He earned a lot more than me. I did secretarial work. I never earned a lot of money.

Betty took Brad to a counsellor who said to him, "'Brad, look at your wife. She's exhausted.'" Brad said, he didn't like the counsellor. Another time, Brad took Betty to the psychiatrist and said, Betty wasn't coping. The psychiatrist said, "She's very brittle but she's fine." Betty went to counsellors for her anxiety and depression, but the two times she went for relationship counselling, her husband said the problem was with her. She did not go to financial counsellors for she managed money well. And he did not think he had a problem.

When Betty's son was at university, he tried to get his father to pay Betty housekeeping. Brad started doing that, but she says,

> But then about every six weeks he'd say, 'I can't give you anything this pay.' And I'd say, 'Brad, I've got water, I've got electricity.' With three kids, it was tight all the time. They all went to Catholic colleges ... I remember the finance fellow ringing me one day and he said to me, 'I can see you are paying the fees, but you're a bit behind ... I can see a pattern that you are sending in $50 every month. He asked, 'What year's your son in?' And I said, 'Second year university.' I was still paying the fees. And I did pay them.

Betty's children, like Betty, are good with money. She says her daughter has just bought a flat in Coburg. The bank manager wanted to see her bank accounts. She had twelve accounts, separated for different kinds of expenditure and savings. Betty says her daughter is 'always ahead. I could never get ahead ... I really thought if I went to work, I would get ahead, but I didn't.'

After her husband's death, the children told her how they had paid for some parking fines and how he had borrowed from them. Her daughter told her they hid the parking fines from her and paid them as university students. Her son told her that when he was at university, his father rang up to meet him over coffee.

> Brad asked his son, 'Have you got any money? I've got to go to the races on Saturday.' He wasn't a big gambler. My son said to him 'Dad, I've only got $60 to last the whole fortnight, I can't give you anything.' Brad said 'right' and said, 'I'll drive you back to Uni.' As he drove along, he said, 'Well there's an ATM so you can give me that money.' He stopped. My son got out, got the money and gave it to him. He lived on pasta for two weeks.

When her husband died, her youngest son found the father had three credit cards with $40,000 owing on them. He was able to negotiate with the banks to settle for 40 per cent of the amount. There was no super left, but there was $20,000 owing to Betty's husband for long service and holiday leave. That went to the banks.

Betty and her children don't know the psychology of it. She still does not know what her husband did with his money. Betty and the children concluded he liked to wine and dine, have new cars. She says,

> None of us can talk about it anymore. We can't work it out. But as my son said, when he was trying to sort things out (after Dad died) 'It was like walking into a filthy kitchen and you just didn't know where to start.'

Everybody eulogised Brad when he died. Her son asked her what she wanted to say. She says, after a long silence, 'I said, "We'll say his life was one long lunch."' They all laughed because Brad was out having lunch all the time. She adds, 'We all loved him. He was so good in other ways.'

Betty discovers she suffered family violence

Eighteen months after her husband died, Betty was helping take notes for students with disabilities. It was a lecture on domestic violence. A counsellor asked, 'What are all the types of domestic violence?' The students said physical and verbal abuse. Someone said, 'financial abuse.' Betty says,

I started to cry, and I couldn't stop. I had to leave the class. The counsellor came out. I said, 'My husband died 18 months ago, and we always had a problem with money. It just hit me then, how bad it was.' She said, 'You've suffered domestic violence.' I said, 'Oh no it wasn't.' She said, 'But it was.'

Betty says 'It was like an epiphany. I telephoned my sister and said I had been suffering domestic violence.' She had not recognised it either. It was good to have a label for what she had gone through. She says, 'I remember saying, "There's a label for alcoholics. There should be a label for financial messing up all the time." But I didn't know it came under domestic violence.'

Betty says she was exhausted being married to Brad for 37 years. Now she has felt herself relaxing. The predictability and regularity of the pension has left her feeling good. She still works a bit which brings in about $300 a fortnight. She says, 'I haven't missed a beat, and it's so easy.'

She lives in a three-bedroom flat she bought with the money left over from the sale of her marital home and help from her brother. For the first time in years, she has bought herself a few clothes. She has eaten out more because she wants to. She plays bridge, saying it is social and it is cheap. Betty says, in the past she would not have spent $8 on cakes because I was coming to interview her. She would have bought a packet of biscuits. She already has what she needs for tonight when her brother comes for dinner. She says, 'It's such a relief. I miss Brad terribly but it's such a relief.'

Betty says she is more herself now. Though she was unable to leave Brad, he sapped her confidence. She was always afraid she will meet someone to whom Brad owed money. If she had her time again, she would not have married Brad. If she had to counsel her daughter to avoid economic abuse, she would tell her to live with the man first. You don't know until you live with a man whether he will run out of money on your honeymoon, whether the dentist's bill will not be paid, or wake up one night and find there is no gas.

She says she has great children. She manages well for the present, but worries about the future. Betty says she told one of her sons,

> I've got a bit of Super, my own Super – but what if I run out? What if I live longer?' He said 'Mum, if you run out, I'll put in $10,000 one year.' My other son said, he will put in '$10,000 the next and we'll take it out of the estate when you die.' You know, they are just so lovely.

11 Heer

She knew she should leave but was in a silent 'cultural bind'

Introduction: The silence of family violence in the joint family

Heer[1], 60, grew up in a three-generation patrilineal joint family in India with her parents and her paternal grandparents. Her father was a calm person. Her paternal grandfather was religious. She says, 'I didn't see any physical violence in my close family or extended family.'

Looking back, she recognises her grandmother was emotionally violent towards her mother. Her grandmother would scream abuse. She says, 'Even if it was verbal violence or suppression, there was violence. But I didn't see that as violence when I was growing up. That was acceptable.' Her mother's sister was divorced. Heer assumes there had been some violence, as it was difficult to get a divorce in the 1960s. But it was not talked about. Her mother's sister's ex-husband would visit with Heer's mother even after the divorce. Everyone thought he was a 'very nice man.'

Heer got married before she turned 18. She moved into her marital home and became part of her husband's joint family. Her father-in-law was physically violent to his wife and son. Afterwards they would patch up, be very 'pally' with each other. The father would apologise to his wife or son. Everybody would go out for dinner. Heer says, 'We never talked about it. It wasn't seen, and it was very embarrassing. You did not discuss it.' Her father-in-law would often say he loved his wife. 'No one even sort of spoke of the domestic violence in the house. No one had the guts to say that what you did was wrong.'

---

1 The names are pseudonyms. Details have been generalised to preserve confidentiality.

DOI: 10.4324/9781003178606-11

Heer thinks her husband stood up for his mother. But 'that didn't stop him from being violent towards me for 25 years.'

Economic suppression was not seen as family violence

Heer was in India for the first nine years of her marriage. As she was not in paid work, she had to ask her father-in-law for money. Her husband's family was well off, so she knew she would get the money if she asked. She may have to explain if she wanted thousands, but she would get it. Heer says, it wasn't as if you had your own money that you could spend without questions being asked.

Heer says, 'I saw that as okay. It was fine because I was getting money, if and when I asked for it. Right?' But Heer did not have the habit of asking. She would get a lot of clothes as gifts from her mother and other relatives. There were always gifts of clothes for festivals. So she did not ask.

The need to ask and explain made her secretive and manipulative about the way she talked of money. She says,

> You learn protective behaviours yourself, when you know this thing is going to flare up. So you don't talk about it ... Now at nearly 60, I see that as an abuse too. Because if you can't say, if you can't even say how you feel, there is some sort of violence there...

Heer's friends and family did not know she was experiencing physical, economic and emotional abuse. 'You don't talk about such things,' she says. It was seen as her problem 'because if I'm being abused that means I'm doing something wrong.' Her husband would threaten that he would leave her at her parents' house, but never did. If they had a fight, he would leave her with her uncle or aunt in the morning and come and get her in the evening.

She says, 'I don't think my mum ever knew. She thought I was living a life of luxury. I get everything I ask for.'

Heer's parents-in-law treated her like a daughter. Her father-in-law spoiled her and the children. Yet they could not stop her husband's violence towards her. Heer's father-in-law supported her continued education after marriage. She completed her bachelors and moved on to do an MA and also a B.Ed. She says getting educated after marriage was 'a big deal' in India those days. After marriage, a woman usually stayed at home, cooked, and went to women's 'kitty parties.'

Her husband was not enthusiastic about Heer continuing her education, particularly when she did her MA in a boys' college. He suspected she was meeting other men. Heer and her husband had an active social life. When they came back, 'I would cop it at home because someone was talking to me and he would ask "Why did you talk? Why did you smile?"'

They migrated as a family to Australia in 1984. Heer's husband's sister sponsored them. Heer became the main earner in the joint family. She got a temporary job at first. But because of her teaching qualifications, she was able to get a permanent job with the government within a year. Her husband became a bus driver and his father was in security.

The physical, economic, and emotional violence continued. It was further fuelled by her husband's need to be in control, to feel he was running the household. At first, he was happy with the money he earned, but later the lower status of his job compared to hers began to rile.

When she would come back from an evening shift at her earlier temporary job at 9 pm, her husband would be waiting for her at the station. In the beginning, she thought it was romantic. But on the way back, the grilling would begin, 'Whom did you see? Did you make friends? How many guys worked there? How many women?'

It became worse when she rose to become a manager. He would say 'You think you are too big ... You are in management, and you think yourself to be this or that, whatever.'

She learned to be quiet. Heer says,

> I wasn't supposed to say that I was earning more, and I was.... He would make sure when he was in public... he would say that he is earning this much. I would think, 'Why does he have to talk about his income?' But basically, he was trying to say that I don't earn a lot less than her.

They were seen as a popular, social couple. Yet, when they got home, the violence started.

The economic abuse worsened. In the beginning, she gave whatever she earned to her mother-in-law as she was the one who was supposed to look after the house. However, her mother-in-law would give the money to her son. 'So basically, it was money for him but via my mother-in-law,' Heer says.

When her father-in-law began earning, their money was theirs. It was Heer and her husband's earnings that ran the house. The money in the household was her husband's money or his family's money. It was not her money.

She talks of the time her father-in-law wanted to buy a house in India. She agreed they send $40,000.[2] She says, 'In those days $40,000 was a big amount ... I said, "Oh yeah. No problem." I never thought I could say no.'

Heer had joint accounts with her husband, but she was not supposed to spend money she had earned. She says, 'I had to ask his permission, like "What do you think? Can I buy this? What do you think?" And he'd be counting. "Oh no, no, no we can't do this, we can't do that." She laughs, saying she learned to lie. It was a survival trick. She would shop during her lunch break. She would 'hide it.' Later, she would take it out and say, 'I bought it a year ago.'

She learned to manipulate. She allowed her husband to think he was in control, that 'he was the boss.' She initiated the idea of buying their home and their investment properties. However, she presented it as his idea, as his sister's idea. When her husband warmed to the notion, she would demur and say, 'Well we have to look at our finances.' Her husband said, 'No, I'll look after that, I am in control. I will be telling you what to buy!' So I said, 'Yeah OK sir. Yes sir.' Her husband or his parents chose the house, the colour scheme. Then her husband not only talked of his income; he also talked of his properties.

Her husband was increasingly insecure. The children were growing up. The grandparents doted on the children and the children got everything they wanted. But they could not stop their son from hitting their grandson. Heer's husband had a fetish that the boy could not walk in the house in his socks. If he did not have thongs on or shoes, he would be beaten. Heer's son told her when he was in his 20s, that as a child he would wear two or three track pants, so that the beating would not hurt so much.

Heer leaves and leaves again

The violence increased, though Heer's father-in-law and mother-in-law would try to intervene. She left with the children and rented a place. But he would go to her daughter's school. He would come around to where she worked. He brought her friends to convince her to go back. Heer resisted. Then his parents intervened, and she went back. The violence increased. 'It was more of a passive aggressiveness, that I left and ... [brought] shame to him. I've brought shame in the community by leaving him. I've become Australian.'

---

2 The money is in Australian dollars.

He continued with his girlfriends. They had a meeting with family and friends about his womanising. When Heer spoke of it, she says, 'He physically assaulted me in their presence. It was really bad. They had to jump in. That was the first time he did it in public. And not just in public, in front of my sisters, my sisters' husbands and his friends.'

She was so badly bashed, that she had to go to hospital. Heer said her husband had beaten her, but the woman at the hospital did not call the police. Heer went to the police station, but the Apprehended Violence Order (AVO) was not in place then. This was before 1995.

Heer knew about family violence, and dealt with it at work. She says,

> I was in a cultural bind myself. I said a few times, 'I am giving lectures and here I am being caught up …' I spoke to a person in the women's department…. She did not know to what extreme it was … She said, 'We cop it. We don't say anything. We do have double standards.' I am educated. We are in a position [where] I am asking clients why they are not leaving. What am I doing? I am in the same situation.

Heer left him again in 1994–1995. She went to the police again and got an AVO against him. He accepted all responsibility. For five years he did not physically abuse Heer or the children, but the financial control continued. 'Everything had to go through him,' she says. Heer says perhaps it was her fault. 'I treated him like a god.' She built him up to everyone she met. Only a few of her friends and colleagues knew she had an AVO against him. Even her mother did not know.

Heer learnt he was going out with one of her distant relatives. When she confronted him, he said, '"How dare you doubt me and your [relative]?" He became very violent and said, "I'm going to kill you."' Her son heard this and told Heer, 'I try to stay awake, right? But if I sleep and he does something, I might not be able to protect you.' He had never fought with his father about it, never. Never argued about it.

That was the breaking point for me. I thought,

> 'Oh my God. God knows what's happening in my son's mind?' He is not even sleeping for my protection. I didn't see myself so much at risk, but he did. Then all of a sudden, my daughter also said, 'You have to make a choice. Either leave him, or we both are moving out because we've had it. We're not going to stand this nonsense in the house. You're copping it, and that's what we're watching.'

Heer says, 'I didn't leave him for domestic violence or financial stress or suppression.' She left because her husband's violence towards her was hurting her children. All this time, Heer had thought the physical violence was hidden as it was behind doors, in their bedroom. Only twice, he had assaulted her in public. She thought the children did not know.

Her daughter was in her early 20s and her son was five years younger. They rented a townhouse. Within a week they moved. Nobody knew. They only took a few things, the children's beds and one cheap lounge set. They left the good things behind. Heer believed they would come back.

Heer's distant relative moved into the marital home. Heer's husband emptied the joint accounts. He stopped paying the installments on the properties. It was then Heer realised all the things she liked in her house were still there. The children went back for one of the four cars that Heer's son used to drive. They also took the mirror they had gifted Heer. But their father came, slashed the tyre of the car, and told the police the children had threatened him.

At the divorce, Heer paid a lawyer $24,000 and managed to get her half share of the properties. She says, she only had her children for support. Heer used to think his parents were very nice to her and was grateful. Now she thinks it was because she was financially supporting them. She says, 'They didn't do anything to protect me.'

Talking about family violence

Heer and her children did their own counselling by talking with each other of their experience of family violence. One or two friends asked, and she told them. Otherwise, it was her husband's story that went around, that she had left him because he was a bus driver; that she was having an affair. One of her friends said,

> You were an ideal couple. We always looked up to you. You were doing so well. You were such a wonderful wife. You respected him so much. You were always telling him how wonderful he is. He used to cook barbeques ... he was very good socially. He was an excellent friend.

Heer did not explain, thinking they would not understand. She did not go to the Sikh temple or other community organisations. She says,

> I knew what I should be doing. I knew what I had not done. I could give an explanation or justification for not doing it for so many years. And copping it.... My excuse ... was, I was in that culture.

I had three younger sisters. Their marriages will be affected... If I told people, I would cop it more. It would be more embarrassing... Now, sometimes I think that is an excuse, for who cares really ... All my sisters have kept in touch with him.... No one has said, [to him] you were wrong.

Heer is now helping other Indian women who have suffered family violence through an Indian community organisation. She says, 'It's very important to recognise it, to talk about it. And even with symptoms of domestic violence.... people don't talk. I didn't talk.'

Heer thinks the community organisation presents a safe, unthreatening place where the women (mainly) can talk. The volunteers are not related to the women who are suffering family violence. There is a sense of trust. They can tell their story, the way they want, and take as long as they need.

There are more supports today. When she migrated to Australia in 1984, it was not possible to get an AVO. She remembers trying to go to a refuge early on, but there wasn't one available.

She felt empowered after she left. She is financially independent and has strong social relationships. She chooses the way she lives and works. She is able to help other Indian women who have suffered family violence. She says, 'It's very important to recognise it, to talk about it.' Even when people recognise the symptoms of family violence, they 'don't talk. I didn't talk.'

12 Bala
A story of torture, survival and empowerment

Introduction

The pain is still raw for Bala,[1] 49. She is sitting in a spacious house with her second husband. Her parents live with her. She is able to help women experiencing family violence through an organisation she and her husband set up five years ago. Bakshi, Bala's second husband sits by her as she speaks of the abuse over four hours in mid-2016. The two-hour interview spills over into a visit over lunch with her parents in their airy kitchen and dining area.

Talking about the sadness and cruelty of her life 20 years before, she continually breaks up. She is surprised that the past abuse still affects her. She knows she is in a good place now. Her daughter and her husband's children are married and settled. She shows me photographs related to family celebrations, to her birthday, visits from the children.

Bala and Bakshi have a spacious home in the southern suburbs of Melbourne with enough room for extended family living and meeting places for their work on family violence. She takes me around the garden of her home, a conference room to host meetings, four bedrooms, a study, and a theatre room. The prayer alcove is just off the living area. There is also a formal lounge. They have help in the kitchen, ensuring Bala's parents can relax.

Bala had an arranged marriage at 21 while she was still doing her Masters. The match was proposed by a person in her family's affinal network. Her family was attracted to the proposal for the groom's family did not want a dowry. This was important to them for there had been a dowry death in Bala's extended family.

---

1 All the names are pseudonyms. Details have been generalised to preserve confidentiality.

DOI: 10.4324/9781003178606-12

Other than this tick in the groom's favour, the courtship did not progress well. Her father had thought there would be a lot of telephone calls between Bala and her fiancé. He had a phone installed in her room. Bala's fiancé did not call once. There was no card, no letter.

Emotional and physical violence came early in the marriage. After the marriage, Bala's family learnt he had inflated his salary. There was no honeymoon, no period of grooming. Her husband went to work from 7 am to 11 pm, every day of the week. She was alone all day in a rented flat on the fifth floor. She was away from her family, in a regional city in north India, without TV, radio, telephone or friends. Her husband did not introduce her to his friends or take her out.

She got pregnant soon after marriage. She needed to have tests for abnormality. He did not take her for the testing. As the date for testing was expiring, she hired a rickshaw at 8 pm and went on her own from the nursing home to the lab and then to the doctor trying to get the test. In India at that time, it was considered abnormal for pregnant women to visit the doctor without the husband or a family member. The lady doctor in her 60s commented it was the first time in her career that a pregnant woman had come alone.

She went to her parents for the delivery of her daughter. Her husband came to see her after a week.

She breaks down. She says, 'I am sorry, I still get a little bit affected. It was a rough ride. He always shouted at me whenever I would give any suggestions and sometimes slap me as well... I didn't think it would affect me.' Despite this, Bala completed her Masters degree.

They left for Africa with a nine-month-old daughter, as Bala's husband got a job there. Seven years later, her first husband abandoned Bala and their daughter. She returned to India, still in her 20s.

Bala met Bakshi, her second husband, in Africa. They married in India and Bala returned to Africa. They and their three children migrated to Australia in the late 1990s. Bala got into teaching and Bakshi made his way up the finance ladder. Their work led them to greater involvement in the community. For the last ten years or so, both have been involved in work relating to family violence.

Economic and emotional abuse

Bala's first husband did not give her any money when they lived in Africa. This was the beginning of full-blown economic abuse. He appropriated her earnings, controlled her expenditure, did not pay for their daughter's education, denied her money for groceries and tried to sabotage her career.

Bala started working as a teacher in an international school in Africa, for she had a graduate degree. She also offered private tutoring in the evening. She says,

> Initially, I didn't even open a bank account. I used to get my salary via a cheque. I used to endorse the cheque in his name and the money used to go to his account. He gave me an ATM card. Once I went to buy groceries and there was no money in the account. Good that I had put some money aside, even when it was a dollar or something at the end of the month. It was enough to buy groceries.

Bala realised she could not trust him with money. He would not look after Bala and their daughter. Even then, it took two years for her to open a bank account in her own name. She began to keep her earnings, but spent all of them on the house and her daughter. She hired a maid, bought her daughter a computer when she was five. They joined a club so that her daughter had friends. But this meant she had no savings.

She says, 'Though I earned, I had no right to spend money.' She installed an alarm system for she was alone at home most of the time, and afraid it was insecure. He was angry and shouted at her for spending all that money. He said, 'You are nothing. No one will come to hurt you.' Sometime later, she heard someone cutting the grill and was able to call security.

Bala was highly regarded as a teacher. She was invited to work at the best school in town to teach A levels. Her husband, as the main work permit holder, had to sign for her work permit. He sabotaged this move by not signing the work permit. It indirectly led to her being arrested. The police came to get her in a van. She heard them say, 'First she is mine.' They took her to a big government building. She was refused bail. She heard them 'discussing they were going to take her underground to the prison.'

Her daughter was four years old at the time. It was five minutes to five and Bala thought she would jump out of a window. Just then the husband of her head of department walked in. He was African, an advocate, and six feet tall. He got her bail and then got in touch with her husband. Her husband further endangered her by taking her over the border. It was only at the advice of a senior professional, Bakshi, who is now her husband, that she was brought back.

The emotional cruelty took many forms. He demeaned her as a woman, treated her as a servant. His actions were meant to hurt, to show he did not care. Bala says, she would meditate and pray every day as she does even today. After her daughter slept, she would go to another room, put on sad music and cry. She learnt later that her daughter used to stand outside the door and hear her. When her daughter was six, she told her father he had 'tortured' her mother.

Bala says there was one time when the flour had finished. Her husband was playing computer games at home. She went in the car and thought she would not go to the safe parking place, but just stop beside the ATM and withdraw money. Five or six men snatched the money from her, and pulled off her gold chain, bruising her. She came back shaken. Bala told the maid to make rice. Her daughter asked what had happened, but her husband just shouted, '*Roti* (chapati), I want roti. You are good for nothing. I always tell you, you are good for nothing. I can't even get roti in this house.' Bala contorts her face, mimicking the way he shouted.

He accused Bala of not keeping a proper house, of not being attractive. He would open the fridge and ask how old the vegetables were. If he heard they were two days old, he would throw them out, repeating to Bala again and again, 'Get out. Get out.' Bala says, she had always thought of herself as beautiful, as a woman who excelled in what she did. Her husband told her she was unattractive, that she was fat, that she did not know how to keep house, that she was 'nothing.'

There were other periods when her husband would not talk to her. If he wanted to say something, he would write her a note. She did not know what had brought this about. At other times, Bala says, her husband 'would always shout at me. If I suggested anything, he would tell me to shut up, saying, "You think you are very intelligent and can give me a suggestion?"'

She often did not know where he was. He went early, came back late. He would not tell her when he was due to return. She didn't know when he was going out of the city to work, or when he would be back. She had a pager – a mobile was very expensive at the time – but he would not use it. As the security situation was bad, she would worry and call his work sites to find out if he was there. She says, 'He will come back and hit me and shout, "Oh, you are spying on me?"'

He would say he was returning from overseas, and she would go to the airport to find he was not there. He would come back two or three days later, saying he had been busy. He would drop her at a shopping mall, then without telling her, would take the car and leave, so that she had to make her way back alone. When she had surgery for a health problem, her husband told the driver to drop her at the hospital. The driver finished work at 5 pm. Her husband did not come to pick her up till 9 or 10 pm. She had to wait for him, for it was unsafe for women to travel alone at night. He told her she was 'Fat, fat, never say beautiful.' He would agree to go out, and when she was all dressed up, he would refuse to go. Later, she developed a social network where she and her daughter went without her husband, saying he was busy. She does not know what brought on this cruelty. His parents came to stay for a year. They were loving to Bala, but made excuses for their son, saying he was stressed. She says even his parents could not change him. He shouted at them too.

Bala did not tell her parents, fearing her father would have a heart attack. She was educated, earning well to be self-sufficient. She did not complain, fearing her divorce will lessen her sister's chances of a good marriage. She also felt it is better for her daughter to have a father. Bala says, 'I just told myself, "This is my life."' It was only when her mother and sister came to stay towards the end of her stay in Africa, they found she had been silently suffering for seven years.

Throughout her marriage, Bala kept a facade, ensuring her daughter was protected, and that she continued to be highly regarded at work. She did not tell any of her 'friends' what was happening to her. She dressed well, and did her work so effectively that the principal used to cite her as an example of a young delicate woman who was able to keep a class of young adult men absorbed in study.

After seven years in Africa, her husband told her, 'I want to get rid of you. I'm getting a very good job offer in Europe and I don't want to carry this baggage with me.' He did not renew the house lease. At the same time, he threatened to hold on to Bala's passport. Bala and her daughter did leave for India on a one-way ticket. She was offered work at another school in the international network of her present school. Her husband began threatening her on the phone when she reached India. Bala's father put a stop to that. Then he came back to India and apologised, pleading for her to come back.

She returned, despite her family's advice, wanting to give him another chance for her daughter's sake. He did not pay for her ticket. She had to sell jewellery to fund the economy class tickets for her daughter and herself. Her husband flew first class, and told her how terrible the food in economy looked.

It did not get any better when she returned. Her husband lost his job. The house, car and furniture were in the company's name. Fortunately, her school said she could work in one of their international schools in India with a house and free tuition for her daughter. She returned to India the second time. She was still in her 20s.

After the interview, I had lunch with Bala and her parents. They have been staying with Bala and Bakshi for the last 13 years. All their daughters are now in Melbourne. Her mother talked of how scared she and her daughter (Bala's sister) were, when they visited Bala in Africa.

They would sleep with their door closed against Bala's husband, and hid their passports from him.

Bala's mother told a man she thought of as her brother to look after her daughter, as she had to leave before Bala. He assured her that he and his Muslim friend would see to it that she got on the plane. Bala stayed with this 'Uncle' when her husband lost his job, house and car. It was he and his Muslim friend who accompanied Bala and her daughter to the airport.

Bala stopped her mother from talking about the past. She said her mother has low blood pressure, and it was not good for her. We spent time seeing the photograph albums of their youngest daughter's marriage last year in India and Australia.

Helping other women for she knows their pain

Bala and Bakshi talk of what they are doing to address family violence with films, consultation and referral, and community work. Bala says, she is now helping other women to retain hope, and become financially sustainable. They have set up financial literacy programs, skill development, education and support networks. Bakshi helps women check their homeownership documents, for often the husband has put the house in his name, and the liability is the wife's. Bala says, women often say, 'My husband alone takes care of everything.'

They have also set up a men's channel, hoping the men will talk out the issues, and recognise that family norms and laws are different in Australia. They have also been receiving calls from seniors.

Towards the end of the visit, Bala again apologises for having become so 'emotional.' Though life is good for her now, she can still feel the pain and loneliness of 20 years ago. She says, she is glad she can help women who have lost hope. It is healing for her. She says,

> I was once a victim ... I have gone through the pain. I can understand them. I know where they are coming from. I know why they are so scared, why they cannot leave the house. They have a kid. They are thinking not only about themselves, and the situation they are in, but they are thinking about a thousand other things. I want to give them my support, my help.

When a woman is raw because of the violence, seeing nothing but desperation ahead, Bala tells her a small part of her story. She wants the woman to know she too can come through it. She wants them to see that like her, their lives can again have meaning.

13 Enid
Talking of money

Introduction

I first met Enid[1] in 2005 when she was 46. I interviewed her for research on consumer credit. I heard how she had been able to educate eight children in Catholic schools, nearly single handedly, on a yearly income of less than $50,000.[2] It made me think we should clone her.

She was a community-based nurse for 27 years. She found that not being able to deal with financial issues and ill-health were connected. In 2005, she was training to work in financial wellbeing services. We happened on each other over the years because of our interest in consumer finance. For this research on family violence 11 years later in 2016, I went to see Enid and her colleague as they were part of an organisation providing services to persons who were experiencing financial abuse.

I botched part of this interview for I could not stop talking of Chitra who suffered family violence (Chapter 8). The family violence services had not served her well after her divorce. The interview became a counselling session as Enid listened.[3] She said Chitra may just have been young and traumatised like her daughter who too had suffered family violence. Then Enid spoke of how it was only listening to other people's stories she realised she herself had suffered economic abuse. We made time for another recorded interview focusing on her experience of family violence.

---

1   The names are pseudonyms. Some details have been generalised to ensure confidentiality.
2   The money is in Australian dollars.
3   Later, I did seek psychological counselling, for I realised I myself was traumatised that Chitra had fallen through the gaps, and failed to receive help from organisations designed to help those experiencing family violence.

DOI: 10.4324/9781003178606-13

Being prudent with money

Enid migrated to Australia with her European parents when she was nine years old. It was a traditional Catholic family for its time. Her father was the main provider, while her mother looked after the home and children. Enid's father gave her mother housekeeping. Each of them had some money for their own interests – he for his aviary and Enid's mother for her handicraft.

Enid says she is like her parents in her values relating to money. As migrants, they learnt to make do with very little. She says, 'I have learnt to be frugal ... We were always brought up with the idea if you don't need something, you don't buy it. I still do that sometimes. I wish I didn't.'

Enid made the money stretch by sewing her clothes and those for her kids. She would also make their jumpers. The children found it hard to resist the lure for branded clothes and shoes when they were young. But they did. She bought food in bulk, made her own bread. She never used disposable nappies. She saved before she spent. Her children too had to learn to save for things they wanted, like mobile phones and clothes. They did without $180 track suits and at times had holes in their shoes.

Enid's priority was to send her eight children to private Catholic schools. She says this decision was not about religion or about private schools. She wanted them to have a rounded education. She felt, 'If you can't give your kids much materially then education is probably the best thing you can give them.' She wanted her children to 'learn about social justice in a wider context and ... question things that are happening around them.'

Enid thinks the Catholic school system has done that. The children have been actively a part of their school's social justice program and think about people who are less fortunate. This has continued as her children have left home, and become more engaged with community issues.

Seeing issues relating to harmful credit in her work, affirmed her choices to save to spend. She is wary of credit. It is important for her to be debt free. She took a mortgage to buy their home and a loan for a large car, and again to get out of a bad relationship. She has a credit card, but uses it seldom, and then only for emergencies. She says, she once bought a new fridge on her Bankcard, but that was because the old fridge would cost too much to repair. She says,

> I don't use credit very often and have always been very reserved in borrowing.... Hence, I rarely buy new things ... Because of the

large family, I have always had to be careful with money, to be conscious not to overspend. I have tried to educate my kids in the same way.

In 2005, Enid said she used cheques and cash. She would take out a set amount and work within that as a budgeting strategy. She used BPay but it went out of her bank account rather than her credit card.

In 2005, Enid said, unlike her own upbringing, she didn't charge her children board. She started work when she was about 15 and was still at school. She says, 'I had to pay half my money to my parents and I had to save the other half of the half. So, I was allowed to spend a quarter on me.' Enid reasons she was not able to provide the extras to her children when they were growing up. They can now spend their money on themselves. However, one of her older children who was working, did choose to pay board when she came back home after a break.

Enid also differed from her parents in that for much of her life she has been the main earner, as well as looking after the children and the home.

Subservience in marriage

Enid's first husband was Irish Catholic. She married young and had her first child at 21. This marriage lasted 20 years. Her husband had a different upbringing. He grew up seeing and experiencing abuse. Money was poorly managed in his family, and so much of the time they lived in poverty. He knew he was not good with money, so was happy for her to manage it.

Both Enid and her husband were working, but they seldom had a dual income. Either her husband was working, or she was working. Her husband had an accident and got a small payout. They put that down for a deposit for their home. But even after he recovered, he chose not to work much. So, they were reduced to one part time income, with Enid becoming the primary earner.

Their money was in a joint account. With eight children there was little money to spare. Enid says, her husband however had a sense of entitlement. He would spend what he wanted without wondering how the household expenses would be met. Reflecting back to this period in 2016, she says she is also responsible for his extravagance, for she enabled it. She told herself he had lived in poverty for so long, so perhaps it was alright for him to spend. She says, she remained subservient for a while, as being a woman and a mother plus a traditional Catholic upbringing made her put herself last.

When her husband's spending threatened to derail the children's education, she moved her money to a separate account. She also stopped having children. When people hear she has eight children, they immediately think it is because she is Catholic. She says, 'I did come to a point in my life where I realised that probably I had more children because it validated our relationship. I didn't feel that I individually on my own was good enough ...'

She says she has not talked of this for 30 years. But after realising that, she made a conscious decision not to have any more children. She was still married. Her husband was unhappy he had lost reproductive control. It is her husband who left. He left to travel interstate and overseas after 20 years of marriage. He came and went for two years. After that, she told him not to come back. He lived overseas for seven years and had a well-paid job. But there was little contact with the children and no maintenance.

She had all eight children at home and for eight months she stayed at home without work. She was dependent on Centrelink benefits. Enid says she did not like that, but it was a 'stable income.' When she went back to work, the money varied every fortnight. She still had her house. They were able to pay for food. But she had to juggle the payments every fortnight. She was able to defer some utility payments. When she got the school bill for $3,500, she waited a while before going to see the bursar. He told her he had dealt with similar situations before. Enid went on a fortnightly payment plan. The money then went out in smaller amounts via direct debit. She continued paying for some years after the school years were over.

She was a single parent for seven years before she went into a relationship. She still had six children at home. She was the main earner, though her partner contributed from his earnings as a tradesperson. He was also mechanically minded and so they were able to manage with old appliances. However, the household income was still under $50,000.

Enid says, 'I repeated the same thing as in my first marriage ... I paid for everything that I consumed, that my children consumed. There was not a sharing of resources.'

Enid again went into a joint account with him, but also had a separate account. While in the relationship, she thought she had found a person with similar values. They bought a house together. But when she left him, he wanted her share of their house. She recognised this as 'absolute financial abuse.' She says, 'He tried to undermine me in ways I did not expect.' She adds,

He lied about his own assets. He did not share money and the system [at the time of settlement] did not take the children into consideration, since they were not his. He had no legal responsibility for them under the law. I was unable to close a joint bank account without his authority and lost some of my money. He coerced me into setting up a new super fund, into which I had put around $3,000, but his financial adviser 'friends' put the fund into his name only – so I lost that.

She also had to borrow $10,000 for legal advice and court fees. It took her two years to get a property settlement. She says, 'During this time I had to rent a house – I was seriously financially disadvantaged.'

When Enid walked out of this relationship, she still had six children at home. She says, 'I remember one day ... I made a conscious decision that ... I do not need this kind of rubbish in my life. I do not need a relationship at all.' It was a personal decision. She did not talk about it. She says she still remembers the day. She had had closure on the property settlement. She says, 'I didn't need to be a victim. I didn't need to be subservient. In my previous relationships ... even though I worked, I was subservient to the person I was in a relationship with.'

She did get married a second time. She says, 'I think I put myself in a much better place to meet someone who was equal in their thinking. My marriage this time is different. We've always equally shared the money.' Both have been single parents. He didn't assume he had rights to anything. Enid and her partner talk about money as they move across life stage, and employment patterns.

In the beginning, both were employed. But in 2016, he was 63 and no longer working at a job. She at 57 was again the primary earner. Her husband works on land they bought, growing fruits and vegetables for the house. She says, 'I make sure money goes into his account every week. We agree what that amount is. If he needs more, we also have a joint account. We talk about it.'

Their children are no longer at home, but both still feel some responsibility towards them. That responsibility is shared. Enid says, 'I had to learn that this person was very happy to share on an equal basis. I had to learn that that was normal.' It had not happened in her life before.

Recognising economic abuse

Looking back at money in her first two relationships, she says she did not see her husband's failure to provide, and to spend without considering the family as 'economic abuse as such ... I thought it was perhaps irresponsibility ... I didn't really know that term in the way that I understand it now.' Economic abuse is not a term they used even in consumer finance till 2014.

She says this failure to speak of and recognise economic abuse is related to gender and upbringing. It also relates to men feeling entitled to money. Women universally put the home and children first. The women themselves come last. She says, 'Traditionally men have earned more, been the primary earner. She adds, 'There was an entitlement and a right to the money as theirs ... I didn't have that.... I thought I would share it because that was how I'd grown up.'

It is women's lack of a sense of entitlement to money and economic resources that translates into professional practice. Economic abuse is not well articulated, because women dominate the community sector. And it is often these community service professionals that first identify family violence.

Speaking for herself, she says her upbringing was such that she felt as a woman she was less entitled, less worthy of goods. 'I have felt you only have exactly what you need, the bare minimum. So, when I got married that was the same. I thought I need food; I need some clothes. But those clothes, I can make them, I can buy them at the op shop.' She says she is still like that, even though for most of her adult life she was the main earner. But now, if she feels she needs a new coat, she will allow herself that.

This change happened when she was on her own for seven years and making all the financial decisions by herself. She says, she is not as austere in refusing herself, but she continues to 'figure out things to suit what my family needs.'

Talking of money in intimate relationships

Enid says part of the problem is that we don't speak of money in intimate relationships across life stages. Often, we don't speak of money at all in the family. Enid says she knew, 'My parents owned their own property.... my father had an overseas pension, and they were pensioners here. That is really all I knew. I didn't know if they had savings.' It was only after her father died, that her mother revealed she had always felt very 'contained' by her husband. This was despite her being a good money manager and organiser. She says, her brother probably knew more. Her father believed it is the male who manages the money. So possibly her brother was more aware of their financial situation and arrangements for funeral costs.

Her parents also did not know about Enid's economic abuse. Enid says, she probably was ashamed to tell them. Her father was very judgmental about her divorce and her subsequent relationship. As a Catholic, he saw both as taboo. Though her second husband is also Catholic, Enid and her father never resolved these issues.

Enid guesses her children knew that money was tight when they were growing up. She hopes they knew their education was a priority, and so they had to do without some things they desired. Her children could see how she had changed in the way she and her second husband dealt with money in their marriage. But when Enid's children were growing up, the talk was about managing and saving money. There was also transparency about money. When her children borrowed from her, they paid her back.

She felt her journey of overcoming economic abuse and moving to a financially equal relationship would fireproof her children, particularly her daughters, against family violence. But two of her daughters did suffer family violence. Her daughters had imbibed what she did when they were growing up, rather than what she said to them later. However, a habit of discussing money and relationships meant they were able to have a conversation about money and relationships, when there was a life stage change. One of her daughters, 22, was earning independently, got married and had a child. Instead of two incomes there was one. Her daughter did not want to ask her husband for money. For a while she managed on the family benefit, but then had to ask him for money. He was surprised for he had never been asked before.

Enid says, it is not conscious abuse. It is just that they had not had a conversation about the impact of having a child, and going from two incomes to one. They had not talked about how they will manage 'my money, our money and your money.' How will this work out at different life stages?

Her daughter had in the first instance accepted the situation, much in the way Enid had done in her first marriage. When her daughter did have that conversation with her husband, things got better. Enid makes the point that when talking of money, what is needed is not so much respect, but an 'unconditional mutual regard' for each other. Respect has a hierarchical aspect, but unconditional mutual regard means you are open to listening to each other.

Enid was surprised her daughter was exposed to economic abuse. She thought that,

> .... just the experience they had with me and the way I changed my life would actually influence her. What I learnt ... was that my subliminal behaviour over the years when they were young, probably had much more impact than I ever realised. As I am getting older,

I think that what children are exposed to in their early years stays in their lives, impacts on their decision-making ability.

Her daughter, 22, confirmed this. She said to Enid, 'Mum how do you expect us to turn out different when we have been watching you do this all these years?' What Enid had thought was good and dedicated behaviour as a wife and a mother, had hurt her daughter. 'She had absorbed what I did, not what I said.' Enid adds, 'The situation is very different now. A great understanding has developed with conversations and open sharing of money.'

14 Conclusion

The lived experience of economic abuse across cultures

The stories show that none of the women fully realised they were suffering family violence through economic abuse, whilst it was happening to them. Two of the 12 recognised it after their marriage was over. One heard of it in a lecture. Another said her friend pointed it out. They were relieved to realise their husband's denial of money, appropriation of assets and sabotaging of paid work was not because they did not know how to deal with money, were incompetent or 'obsessive.' Economic abuse was the way their husbands exercised coercive control to isolate, entrap, and diminish them.

Coercive control is a malicious pattern of abuse to remove a woman's freedom and human rights. As detailed in Chapter 1, it follows a pattern that starts with grooming, leading to coercive behaviour and ends with a debilitating impact on the victim. For some of the women in the stories, the grooming stage was short and coercive behaviour started nearly immediately after marriage.

The impact of coercive control was traumatic and devastating. The women spoke about the abuse being 'torture' and 'slavery.' They did not know when the horror would begin. More than one woman talked of 'walking on eggshells.' One woman tried to commit suicide three times. Another was suicidal. The women feared they were going crazy and losing their sense of self. Some women speaking 20 years after the abuse, broke down. It was difficult to relive the pain.

The stories illustrate the gendered nature of coercive control. It was gendered for it was the men abusing the women, and the abuse itself targeted gendered roles. The husband accused his wife of 'not being a good wife,' not being able to cook, being unattractive, not knowing how to deal with money.

Conclusion 99

These were not just occasional disagreements about spending and savings. It was a repeated pattern of abuse, making her fearful, convincing her she was to blame for her lack of freedom and choice. The economic abuse was about denying the woman money, appropriating her assets, and sabotaging her work or ability to work. Economic abuse meant the man did not provide, did not fulfil his moral role as a husband to ensure the family's welfare. It meant monitoring and questioning the woman about every item of expenditure. He spent the money he earned on 'men's toys', leaving his wife and children to do without.

Among the Indian women, economic abuse was all of this and more. Economic abuse meant the husband sent all his money – and sometimes some of his wife's money, without consultation – to his parents in India so the wife had to do three jobs to make ends meet. It was pressuring her family to give him and his family, money and gifts – first through dowry and then continued through demands of money and property. In some cases, the husband's natal family also became perpetrators of continual economic, emotional, and physical abuse. If the husband's family kept the woman's jewellery to 'safeguard' it, she never got it back. In two cases, the jewellery was stolen by the husband as he left.

Coercive control was more easily used over migrant women who did not have networks of family and friends in the country. Monitoring, controlling, or taking away the mobile phone and preventing the use of the Internet, were powerful ways of denying the woman contact with her family overseas, and the world outside her home in Australia. Some women were persuaded to open joint accounts, so that the husband could monitor the wife's expenses and take her money. The husband could argue this is the Australian way, and would help in proving a genuine relationship when applying for permanent residence.

The stories show that Australian migration law, misinterpreted, itself becomes a form of abuse. In more than one Indian story, the husband told the woman on a temporary visa, she would be deported if she did not obey him and his family. This is frightening for a woman for if she is on a temporary non-partner visa she doesn't have any protections. Even if she is on a temporary partner visa, she most likely does not know that a woman can get permanent residence without her husband's sponsorship if there is evidence of family violence.

The women in these stories did not foresee economic abuse. Where the woman was expecting jointness and togetherness regarding money, she found she had to battle alone to keep the family fed. Even when the woman was the main earner, the man felt entitled to spend her money, while abusing her emotionally, and sometimes physically. Even when the woman was openly looking for some measure of autonomy, her husband continued to feel a sense of entitlement about her money.

Some women recognised they were experiencing control and male entitlement. One recognised financial abuse when her partner wanted to appropriate her assets. But none of the women named it as family violence. Even if they had done so, the law offered little help. Family violence law in Australia – except for Tasmania – does not treat economic abuse as a crime. At present, the Australian legal system tells women in an intimate relationship that it is criminal if the man beats you. But it is not a crime for him to deny you money, appropriate it, sabotage your work, and push you and your children into poverty.

The women's experience was that none of the perpetrators of economic and emotional abuse apologised. None of them were prosecuted. In some cases, despite the violence they unleashed, they were successful in getting more than half the house, even when they had not contributed equally towards it. They were able to deny child support, hound women through the courts, adding to the trauma already suffered. The women were left thinking the state had become an actor in the continuation of the violence of money.

The medium of care becomes the medium of abuse

It is difficult for women, practitioners and persons involved in the legal system to recognise economic abuse because money as a medium of care can become the medium of abuse.

Middle-income Anglo-Celtic couples in Australia see the joint bank account as a symbol of togetherness and partnership in marriage. It is the way they signal to themselves and to others that they are a married couple. It is such an accepted part of money in marriage, that having a joint account is one of the ways migrant couples can officially evidence they have a genuine intimate relationship. This symbolism and ideology of partnership that accompanies the joint account, makes it difficult to anticipate or accept that the joint account can also be a medium of abuse.

Many stories in this book show the joint account becomes a medium of abuse when it is used mainly to hold the woman's money. The man keeps his money separate and does not provide. The joint account then gives the man the ability to withdraw and spend the woman's money while monitoring her expenses. So even when the woman is the main earner, she may have no access to her money and be afraid to ask for it or spend it.

Having a separate account while earning substantially less than the man, also does not protect the woman. If the husband does not share the expenses for the household and children, the woman is left to struggle with all the expenses on a lesser income, while he spends all his earnings as he wishes.

In the migrant Indian community in Australia, remittances – money sent home – are a medium of care for the family left behind. It is a moral expectation particularly for the sons and is part of the cultural intergenerational sharing of money. However, if the man sends all his earnings and some of his wife's money – without consultation – remittances become abusive. They siphon money away from his wife and children, leaving them with little for settlement and everyday expenses. The man is a 'moral son' for sending money home, but is an abusive husband and father depriving his wife and children of money for essential expenses.

Control becomes coercive when it betrays the morality of money

The way money is managed and controlled by itself does not predict economic abuse. These different money management and control systems become coercive when they betray the accompanying morality of money. This is an important insight for policy makers and practitioners who worry about drawing the line between what is normally accepted in a culture and what is abusive. Recognising this insight also prevents seeing money practices in other cultures being abusive just because they differ from money practices in your culture.

Economic abuse is seen in money management systems that are joint, separate or independent. The women in the stories in this book managed money through joint accounts, separate accounts or a combination of joint and separate accounts. One migrant Indian woman deposited her money in her husband's account in the beginning. Some women believed in the jointness of money in marriage while others were comfortable with the male control of money. Yet, husbands used money to control the women's lives, entrap and isolate them; and made them feel this was happening to them because it was their fault.

These money management and control arrangements can be unequal, but the person controlling the money is expected to use the money for the welfare of the family. It is when control is exercised without responsibility and morality, with an intent to harm the partner, children, and other members of the family, that control becomes coercive.

The joint account is not abusive by nature. It becomes abusive when it is not accompanied by a sense of partnership and togetherness. A separate account in marriage also comes with the expectation the man will provide. Similarly, remittances become a medium of coercive control when they are used to deny the woman essential money to run the household, and look after the children.

As detailed in Chapter 1, the changing gender of money because of women's increased paid work, migration, and changing ideologies of marriage leads to moralities from a previous era coexisting with present moralities. These conflicting moralities need to be sensitively negotiated. One of the stories tells of an Anglo-Celtic woman now in her 60s, who started marriage with a joint account. She was in paid work, but she gave up this work when her first child was born. She subscribed to the traditional expectation that the woman looks after the home and children, and the husband provides. They continued to have a joint account. But the husband did not provide consistently. He was in and out of work. Even when he had a business, he did not contribute regularly to the household expenses, choosing to spend his money on 'men's toys.' Economic abuse resulted because the moralities related to money had been violated. This couple was not able to keep the aura of joint money, nor did the husband provide. The wife and children were pushed into poverty.

Migration triggers the same clash of moralities because of the changing gender of money. The Indian women in the stories have graduate and professional education and were in paid work before or/ and during marriage. They are also exposed to the Australian norm of jointness in money in marriage. The women expected jointness with some autonomy. Some also wanted to send money home to their parents. But the women in the stories found themselves trapped, when the husband continued to subscribe to the traditional morality of money, where the wife's earnings belong to him and his natal family.

Surviving economic abuse

The stories are searing accounts of family violence, but they are also empowering stories of surviving economic abuse.

Not surprisingly, these stories show it is easier if a woman gets out fast from an abusive relationship. The longer a woman remains under coercive control, the more she sees herself through the eyes of her abuser. She begins to lose confidence in her own ability. Her personality changes. Younger women left faster – within one to three years – than the older women who at times were in a relationship for 20 years

Conclusion 103

or more. For five of the 12 women, it was the husband who left the relationship. One husband died. In two instances, the husband left, abandoning the wife and children. In another case, the husband began a relationship with another woman. In the fifth case, the husband suggested divorce.

Leaving an abusive relationship remains difficult and dangerous. But younger women are better able to leave and leave earlier in the marriage, because there is a greater awareness of family violence and the existence of support services. The older women at times had no options to leave. They also continued in their relationship because of religious and social norms around the sanctity of marriage. They feared negative effects on their natal family if they left the marriage. The stories show women who have experienced family violence more recently have found more support from friends and family than women who suffered family violence years ago. However, it continues to remain difficult for women to tell their families and friends they are suffering economic and emotional abuse. They are ashamed it is happening to them. They still see it as a personal issue rather than a social problem.

The Anglo-Celtic women who told their stories were older than most of the Indian women. The Anglo-Celtic women whose parents had been alive when they had suffered abuse talked of how their parents and priests said, 'You made your bed. You lie on it.' This reaction made the woman feel even more isolated. Older Indian women did not tell their parents, trying to prevent their parents and siblings from getting hurt. For nearly all the younger Indian women, parents' and sibling support was fast and unwavering. In the one case where the woman did not talk of her parents' help, the abusive marriage had sundered her relationship with her natal family.

Education provides a starting point for survival. However, it is the continuity of paid work which gives a woman the confidence she can survive and support her children. Paid work is so important for resilience that one of the ways a woman is economically abused is to prevent her from being employed. Women who have had a long break in their paid work have had to spend years retraining or must start again in work that offers less money and status.

It is important for women to know of and use the professional, financial and settlement services that are available to help survivors of family violence. This presupposes the women have recognised they have suffered family violence, and that money has been part of that violence. These services can help a woman flee from family violence. They can help a woman devise a safety plan and help use the recent policy instruments that are meant to help with housing, counselling, visa issues, financial support, coerced debt, rented property and utilities. Even then, a woman may find herself falling through the cracks. But these services can also turn a woman's life around.

One of the stories told of a young professional Indian woman so traumatised by the abuse she had suffered, that her first reaction was to return to India where she had family support. She had no friends and no work in Australia. Her only memories of Australia were of torture. But after community leaders referred her to professional multicultural services, she was granted permanent residence and received valuable counselling. She regained her confidence. Her parents sent her $500[1] in the first month to help. Her presentation, education and previous managerial experience ensured she had a job in a month and a half. She now sees Melbourne as her city and home.

The relational literacy of money

It is usual to hear of the importance of increasing a woman's financial literacy and capacity when she leaves an abusive marriage. This is particularly relevant to women from refugee backgrounds who may not be fluent in English and have not dealt with banking.

All of us can use more financial literacy at different stages of our lives. But the women in the stories in this book had professional or graduate education. Ten of the twelve were in paid work before marriage. Six of the 12 women were the main earners in their marital households. They may have lacked money after they left the marriage, but these women did not lack financial literacy or capability. They were subjected to economic abuse which involved coercive control. Their education and paid work helped them survive economic abuse, but did not prevent it.

The stories in this book point to supplementing financial literacy with what I term the *relational literacy of money*, for both men and women. It involves communicating and listening to your partner about each other's experience of money, negotiating joint and personal money at each life stage, and sharing these insights with your children.

This concept draws on the women's reflections about talking of money and family violence. It was after the women left their marriage, that some began to talk about money and family violence with their children and other women. Family violence – if it had occurred in

---

1   The money is in Australian dollars.

their families – used to be shrouded in silence. They hoped talking of subjects that were taboo before, may help their children and others speak more openly, and live a life free of violence.

This was new behaviour and part of a major social change. None of the women learnt from their parents how to speak of money in intimate relationships. They had however observed how their parents dealt with money. Some women in these stories knew whether their mothers had to ask for money, whether they had separate incomes and accounts. They also knew whether their parents had a troubled or respectful relationship around money. Some women learnt to expect the husband to provide, be frugal, and put their own needs last. Others intentionally wanted to manage money differently from their mothers. They wanted more independence and responsibility around money than their mothers had, or chose to have.

There are some resources that can help us talk about money in intimate relationships to prevent economic abuse within and across cultures. In Australia, an information and support service for women has an important online resource entitled *Women Talk Money* (Women's Information and Referral Exchange Inc (WIRE), No year stated). It covers the issues related to money, gender and relationships, and principles around talking about money in intimate relationships. There are also advice columns dealing with conflicts around money in intimate relationships. Psychologists and counsellors who counsel couples and families have important insights about money. Memoirs around money can be perceptive (Morton, 2020; Perle, 2006; Pritchard, 1999). I have also found books dealing with gendered differences in communication to be transformative in the way we talk about money (Tannen, 1990).

The first step in the relational literacy of money is being able to communicate and listen with understanding and empathy to how you and your partner have grown up with money. It also means exploring how you want to deal with different kinds of money, such as earnings, savings, expenditure, personal money, joint money, remittances and family money in your intimate relationship.

One of the 12 women talked of her story of money before her first marriage, and another before her second. The woman who tried talking to her partner before her first marriage later found she had not been heard. I do not know whether her partner told her his story of money. These two women also spoke of how they would balance joint and personal money. The marriage of the first woman ended within two years, before she had children.

The second woman learnt from her previous marriage and relationship that she did not want to live in a relationship where she was subservient around money. She and her future husband talked of their stories of money before marriage. They continued to negotiate the balance of joint and personal money in an atmosphere of 'mutual regard' across life stages.

It can be awkward to talk of money in intimate relationships, fearing it will lead to conflict. There are cultural ways of preventing talk of financial dependence and independence. The joint account is itself a secular ritual to speak of togetherness and jointness, rather than power, financial dependence, earnings, and discretionary expenditure. In India, questions by the wife about her husband's earnings can be seen as intruding into his male sphere (Singh, 1997; Singh & Bhandari, 2012). But if the couple is hoping for partnership in their relationship, it is a red flag if they cannot speak of money. Talking of money with a future partner is an important sign of open communication and mutual regard.

Conversations about money and relationships have an intense intimacy. Hearing how a person has grown up with money or without, how his or her parents dealt with money, gives you a privileged look into his or her life and family. Talking of money lets a person talk of other more unspoken aspects of life, such as the kind of life they want to live, the person they hope to become. If a person's story of money remains untold, each partner may take different kinds of money for granted. The women's stories show when the pattern diverges from their expectations, both may feel wronged.

Talking about money is important for we often take for granted the gender and morality of money. The moral norms around money are not articulated. A conversation about the gender and morality of money is particularly important before committing to an intimate relationship, because many of the sureties of the gender and morality of money in our parents' generation have changed. These changes are even more profound with migration, where the couple is faced with different cultural models of money in intimate relationships. As one of the stories shows, these changes in the gender of money may be uneven for men and women. Men may not have questioned their father's sense of entitlement as much as women have questioned their mother's dependence.

The second aspect of the relational literacy of money is that conversations about money need to periodically negotiate the balance of personal and joint monies across life stages. These conversations should be held with 'unconditional mutual regard,' as one of the women said.

In these stories, having a child was often the first major change to the ownership, management, and control of money. Most of the women in the stories were in paid work before marriage and children. Some of the women gave up paid work to look after the home and children. None discussed the short and long-term effects of giving up paid work on their present and future financial resilience, and the balance of personal and joint moneys. Two of the women addressed this change through part time or lower paid work. None of the women negotiated a direct credit into their personal account or their partner's account, so that there continued to be personal and joint monies, though the balance could have changed.

As one of the women found, retirement of one partner or both is also a life-stage that changes the balance of 'my money,' 'your money' and 'our money.' Without a salary coming in, will the pension or benefits suffice? This is an important question to ascertain the adequacy of household income. But for the partners it is also important to ask: How does each partner get his or her money for personal expenditure? It is important to talk about it, to discuss how much they need for joint expenses, how much they want for their continuing obligations towards their adult children, and how much each want for themselves. It is easy then to organise a direct credit to the partner's account so that it does not feel like a hand-out.

The same kind of discussion needs to happen with migration where the migrating partner often needs to rebrand herself/himself or retrain to pursue their former professional occupation. This means the more settled partner has to accept a period where he/she will have to provide for all the household and personal expenses, while the other partner prepares to work in a new country. If the couple is from the global South, an important conversation needs to be had about remittances sent to their families in the source country. How do they balance their settlement needs with the morality of sending money home?

The third aspect of the relational literacy of money is to discuss your insights with your children. None of the women in the stories had their parents talk to them of money as they grew up. They observed how their parents managed and controlled money, but they did not have a conversation about money and relationships. These women in turn did not talk of money and relationships with their children while they were in the abusive relationship. One woman had to learn how to talk of money with her daughter when she found her daughter was in danger of suffering economic abuse. Though the woman herself was now in an equitable relationship with her second husband, her daughter was following the mother's behaviour in her previous economically abusive relationship.

Her daughter had learned from her mother how to be prudent and transparent with money. But she had also learned not to express her own needs in terms of money and continued to put herself last. When the daughter had a child, she stopped paid work. She had never asked for money in her marriage. Her husband had never had to provide. They had not discussed who would be responsible for expenses, or how each partner would have personal money. They had not negotiated the balance of personal and joint money, present and future money. At this point, the mother was able to suggest that money needs to be negotiated and re-negotiated at different life stages with a sense of 'unconditional mutual regard,' rather than a sense of entitlement.

Proposals for policy and practice

The women's stories have important messages for policy and practice. These address the importance of criminalising control so that economic abuse is seen as a crime. It is important to budget significant resources for the training of legal professionals to recognise, prosecute and judge coercive control. Providers of family violence services also need to be trained to recognise and learn about the gender and morality of money across generations and cultures. This helps them recognise the red flags of economic abuse. Major social change about increasing awareness of money and control in relationships can take place by learning to reflect and speak about money in our intimate relationships with mutual regard.

The women's stories show they were not aware that economic abuse is family violence. Criminalising coercive control can help send a clear message that society does not condone domestic physical and non-physical abuse, that family violence of any kind is a social problem and not a private shame. This message is educative and can raise awareness of the nature and prevalence of economic abuse. Naming of the abuse can enable the woman, with help from family, friends, and support services, to prepare to leave if she wants to, and if she can. She can begin preparing for financial resilience, so that she and her children have a future.

Criminalising coercive control means budgeting significant resources for training legal professionals to increase their capacity to recognise, investigate, and prosecute coercive control. Legal personnel need training to move from the 'violent incident model' to a narrative of physical and non-physical abuse. The training needs to enable them to understand the nature and 'thresholds' of coercive control that diminish a woman's autonomy and ability to leave. Gender sensitivity is essential, as coercive control is gendered in nature and nearly wholly perpetrated by men. This training will be complex. But as Wiener says, 'a criminal offence cannot be overlooked because it is complicated' (Wiener, 2017).

Providers of family violence services also need to focus on economic abuse. A focus on the changing gender of money and morality within and across cultures emphasises the need to learn and listen particularly to women from new migrant and refugee groups. This will generate trust between service providers, particularly when they are of a different culture from the clients. It can increase these women's access to family violence services, while at the same time strengthening the service provider's ability to assess risk in a culturally sensitive manner. It can also help increase multicultural and multilingual staff in these services, so that culturally and linguistically diverse (CALD) women can be assured they are being heard and understood.

Major social change can happen when we begin to have trusted conversations about money and relationships. Most of us are not taught how to talk about money in a way that articulates our needs. It is important to learn from each other how to speak of money in terms of relationships rather than quantum. We need to learn from each other of conversations about money that have failed and to what effect, and conversations about money that have built up trust and togetherness in intimate relationships.

There is no single way to write a primer on the relational literacy of money. No conversation about money is the same as another, for it is rooted in biography and culture. But we learn from some of the women's stories that these conversations are most powerful between parents and children. Each person most likely assumes his/her parents' behaviour around money is the 'proper' way to deal with money in intimate relationships. It is important to talk of money with your future partner for his/her template may not be the same.

It is also important to negotiate at every life stage change how both can deal with money that will be used for joint expenses and savings, and money put aside for each partner. Migration, having children, unemployment, caring for parents, helping adult children settle, and retirement – these life stages often change the amount of money available. The balance of personal and joint money can change. When the change comes with consultation, it can increase the jointness of intimate relationships.

The women who told their stories hoped for change. These proposals for changes in law, practice, and communicating money can help strengthen relationships, and prevent the devastation of economic abuse.

References

Morton, R. (2020). *On Money*. Sydney: Hatchette Australia.

Perle, L. (2006). *Money, A Memoir*. New York: Henry Holt and Co.

Pritchard, R. (1999). *How Money Comes Between Us*. Auckland: Tandem Press.

Singh, S. (1997). *Marriage Money: The Social Shaping of Money in Marriage and Banking*. St. Leonards, NSW: Allen & Unwin.

Singh, S., & Bhandari, M. (2012). Money management and control in the Indian joint family across generations. *The Sociological Review*, *60*(1), 46–67.

Tannen, D. (1990). *You Just Don't Understand: Women and Men in Conversation*. Milsons Point, NSW: Random House Australia.

Wiener, C. (2017). Seeing what is 'Invisible in Plain Sight': Policing coercive control. *The Howard Journal of Crime and Justice*, 1–16. doi:10.1111/hojo.12227

Women's Information and Referral Exchange Inc (WIRE). (No year stated). *Women Talk Money*. Retrieved from https://www.womentalkmoney.org.au/

Index

Adams, A. E. 3, 4, 5, 16
Akuei, S. R. 11, 14, 16
Alhabib, S, 6, 16
Anglo-Celtic: definition 1n1; marriage as a partnership 12, 25, 100; money belongs to the couple 13; money not a preferred gift 12; one-way flow of money 12, 13; privacy of money 1; *see also* joint account
Apprehended Violence Order (AVO) 43, 44, 61–62, 81
Australian Bureau of Statistics 1, 3, 16, 37
Australia's National Research Organisation for Women's Safety (ANROWS) 4, 18, 19

Bandelj, N. 10, 16, 23
bank accounts and coercive control 10, 25, 28, 37, 38, 42, 43, 63, 66, 80, 86, 92, 93, 99, 100–102; *see also* joint account
Barwick, K. 1, 16

Carling, J. 14, 17
causes of family violence 5, 7, 49, 52, 75, 88; gender inequality 4; male entitlement 7, 99, 100; patriarchal domination 4, 7
coercive control xi, 6, 9, 98, 9–10; and brainwashing 26; criminalising 6, 8–10, 16, 100, 108–109; gender and 6, 7, 9, 36–37, 98, 109; and homicide 4, 6; narrative of behaviour over time 7–8, 9, 99; in 'other' communities xii; stages of 7–8, 25, 41, 98; tactics of 96–7, 9, 26–27, 36, 68, 98, 99; technology and 2, 8, 32, 33, 35–36, 41, 42, 58, 59, 84, 86–87, 99; *see also* economic abuse, family violence, money
COVID-19: and economic abuse xii; and remittances 14

Dobash, E. R. and Dobash, R. 4, 9, 17
Douglas, H. 5, 9, 17
dowry 32, 33, 34, 35–36, 58–59, 84; as economic abuse 2, 99; *see also* Indian

economic abuse xi, 1–3, 99–100; across cultures 9–10; after separation 3, 4–5, 15, 45, 69, 93–94, 100; among CALD communities 3, 5; and coerced debt 5, 61, 62; gambling as 2, 66; gendered stereotypes 36–37, 60, 87, 98; leaving the home and marriage 4, 5, 28–29, 33–34, 38–39, 50, 56, 61, 72–73, 76, 80–82, 88–89, 102–103; lived experience of xi, 15, 25–28, 32–33, 35–38, 41–45, 46–49, 54–56, 59, 60–61, 70–75, 78–80, 85–89, 92–94, 98–100; measurement of 3; medium of care becomes the medium of abuse i, 10, 25–26, 28, 32, 99, 100–101, 102; not recognising xii, 1–2, 45, 50, 75–76, 78,

94–95, 98, 100; prevalence of xii, 3–4, 10; tactics of 3–4, *see also*, coercive control, family violence, migration, money, morality of money, remittances, surviving economic abuse
emotional abuse 3, 15, 36–39, 42, 44, 56, 59–60, 79–80, 85, 86–88, 99; *see also*, economic abuse

family violence: family history of 63–64, 77; and gender 4; impact on physical and mental health xi–xii, 5–6, 15, 26–27, 33, 42, 54, 66, 67, 70, 71, 72–73, 74, 76, 98, 102; as intimate terrorism 4; legal definition of 1; popular conception of 1, 6, 50, 100; prevalence of 4; silence about 77, 78; as situational couple violence 4; as violent resistance 4; *see also* causes of family violence, coercive control, economic abuse, joint account, migration, remittances
financial abuse 3, 100; *see also* economic abuse
Finch, J. 15, 17

Gamburd, M. R. 12, 18
George, S. M. 12, 18
gender of money xi, 10–11, 14, 25, 49, 54–56, 79–80, 91–93, 95, 102, 106, 102; changes 12–13, 25; and economic abuse 11, 12–14, 54–56, 64–65, 102; and remittances 13–14

Indian: family boundary of money 13; intergenerational flow of money 11, 13, 14–15, 53–55, 101; money as a medium of care 13, 101; money as a preferred gift 12, 13; *see also* economic abuse, joint account, remittances

Johnson, M. P. 4, 18
joint account: and abuse 25–26, 33, 38, 46, 47, 61, 92, 100; and marriage 12, 25, 29, 74, 100; and migration 38, 61, 99, 100; as protection 13; as a secular ritual 106

joint family 12, 13; and economic abuse 10, 15, 59–61, 77–78, 79–80, 82, 99, *see also* Indian

Kurien, P. A. 12, 18
Kutin, J. 3, 18

Lindley, A. 14, 18
Littwin, A. 5, 18
Lukes, S. 2, 18

McMahon, M. and McGorrery, P. 6, 9, 17, 18, 19, 20, 21, 23
management and control of money 2, 10–11, 12, 25, 46, 48, 66, 71, 73–74, 79–80, 91–93, 99, 101–102; and economic abuse i, 37, 42, 46–48, 54–56, 66, 70–72, 78–79, 85–86, 92–93, 101
migration: and economic abuse 2, 5, 37, 41–42, 60, 65, 79, 99, 102, 106; and marriage 31–32, 36, 41, 58; *see also* visas
money: intergenerational flow of 12–13, 53, 55–56; medium of care and abuse 11–12, 32; social and cultural shaping of 10; *see also* economic abuse, family violence, gender of money, morality of money, relational literacy of money
morality of money xi, 11–12, 13–14, 25, 29, 32, 47–48, 71, 74–75, 98, 101–102, 106; and economic abuse i, 25, 32, 47–48, 70–72, 86, 92–93, 99, 100–102

Neave, M. 9, 19
Nyman, C. 2, 19

Olsberg, D. 13, 19
Our Watch 4, 19

Pahl, J. 2, 10–11, 19
Parreñas, R. S. 12, 19
physical assault 60; criminalisation of 1; and economic abuse 1, 4, 6, 15, 27, 36, 37, 38–39, 42, 43, 44, 50, 56, 60–61, 66, 80–81, 85, 99; seen as family violence 6;

violent incident model 8; *see also* economic abuse, family violence, coercive control
police 39, 42–45, 61–62, 66, 67, 81
Postmus, J. L. 3, 5, 6, 20, 22
Powell, A. 8, 20
power: as decision making 2; money as xi, three dimensions of 2
proposals for policy and practice xi, 108–109

Rahman, M. M. 12, 20
Ratha, D. 14, 20
relational literacy of money 104–108; and financial literacy 104; as major social change xi, 105, 109; negotiating personal and joint money across life stages 54–55, 106–107, 109; talking about remittances 54–55, 105, 107; talking of money and family violence i, xi, xiv, 1, 51–52, 69, 82–83, 89, 95–97, 104–105, 106; talking to children 107–108; talking to partners 54–55, 94, 105–106, 109; *see also* surviving economic abuse
remittances 14; as economic abuse 32, 53, 55, 66, 99, 101; as one of the largest international flow of funds 14; as a medium of care 101, as a moral good 11, 14, 32, 101; range of recipients 14; scripts for 14; *see also* economic abuse, Indian, relational literacy of money
reproductive violence 15, 65, 66; *see also* economic abuse

Segrave, M. 5, 8, 18, 20
sexual abuse 3–4; *see also* economic abuse
Sharp, N. or Sharp-Jeffs, N. 3, 5, 6, 20, 21, 25
Singh, S, xiii, 11, 12, 13, 14, 21, 25, 30
sociology/sociologists of money i, xi, 1–2, 10–14
Stark, E. 7, 9, 21, 26, 30

State of Victoria Royal Commission into Family Violence 2, 4–5, 6, 21, 22, 29, 30
Stylianou, A. M. 3, 5, 20, 22
Straus, M. A. 4, 22
surviving economic abuse 1, 15, 28–29, 52, 102–104; continuity of paid work 28–29, 33–34, 50, 56, 62, 67, 88, 103; empowerment xiv, 15, 39–40, 51–52, 56–57, 69, 76, 83, 89, 103–104; faith communities and 28–29, 45, 48, 57, 67, 82, 94, 103; financial fragility 15, 45, 62, 76; friends and family 28–29, 32–34, 39–40, 42, 44, 49, 56–57, 61–62, 67, 73, 76, 87–88, 103; further education and reskilling 50–51, 60–61, 69, 103; help from support organisations 3, 39, 41, 43, 44, 45, 61–62, 67–68, 83, 103–104, 109; leaving fast 28, 33–34, 39, 56, 102–103; remarriage 29, 82, 85; work place 32–33, 39, 67; *see also* relational literacy of money
Surviving Economic Abuse 5, 22

Tolmie, J. R. 9, 22
Tuerkheimer, Deborah 9, 22

Vaughan, C. 3, 6, 22
VicHealth 4, 6, 19, 22
visas: marriage and permanent residence 31, 33, 34, 63, 65; temporary 5, 60, 99; *see also* Indian, economic abuse
Vogler, C. 2, 11, 22

Walklate, S. 9, 22
Wangmann, J. 9, 10, 22
Webster, K. 6, 23
Wherry, F. F. 7, 10, 11, 16, 23
Wiener, C. 7–8, 23, 109, 110
Wilkis, A. 11, 23
writing the stories xii–xiv, 15; ethics of xiii

Zelizer, V. A. 10, 11, 14, 16, 23